SOUP FOR EVERY MEAL . . .

Breakfast . . .

APRICOT YOGURT SOUP (CHILLED)

Creamy, beautiful orange, and sprinkled with coconut, a wonderful change from plain old juice or half a grapefruit.

Lunch . . .

SORREL SOUP

Known as *Potage Germiny* by the French, it is the *pièce de résistance* for a light special luncheon . . . served with salad and crusty French bread.

Dinner . . .

BAKED CARIBBEAN FISH SOUP

The perfect first course for a fiesta-style dinner, it has a definite chili zing and a delicate blend of background flavors.

After-Theater Snack . . .

OYSTER BISQUE

Taking no longer than five minutes to prepare, this dish is elegant, spontaneous, and sure to get rave reviews.

THE ULTIMATE SOUP BOOK

JULIA OLDER has written, along with STEVE SHERMAN, three previous cookbooks: *Soup & Bread; Cheese, Sweets, Savories;* and *Menus à Trois: The Soup, Bread, and Salad Cookbook*. Also the author of five nonfiction books and two poetry collections, she has been a fellow at the MacDowell Colony in New Hampshire. STEVE SHERMAN is the author of twelve nonfiction books, including *Wreaths for All Seasons*.

THE ULTIMATE
SOUP BOOK

250 Soups for
Appetizers, Entrées, and Desserts

Julia Older and Steve Sherman

Ⓟ
A PLUME BOOK

PLUME
Published by the Penguin Group
Penguin Books USA Inc., 375 Hudson Street,
New York, New York 10014, U.S.A.
Penguin Books Ltd, 27 Wrights Lane,
London W8 5TZ, England
Penguin Books Australia Ltd, Ringwood,
Victoria, Australia
Penguin Books Canada Ltd, 2801 John Street,
Markham, Ontario, Canada L3R 1B4
Penguin Books (N.Z.) Ltd, 182-190 Wairau Road,
Auckland 10, New Zealand

Penguin Books Ltd, Registered Offices:
Harmondsworth, Middlesex, England

First published by Plume, an imprint of New American Library,
a division of Penguin Books USA Inc.

First Printing, September, 1991
10 9 8 7 6 5 4 3 2 1

 Registered Trademark — Marca Registrada

LIBRARY OF CONGRESS CATALOGING IN PUBLICATION DATA:

Older, Julia, 1941–
    The ultimate soup book : 250 soups for appetizers, entrées, and desserts / Julia Older and
Steve Sherman
        .p   cm.
    ISBN 0-452-26609-2
    1. Soups. I. Sherman, Steve, 1938–   . II. Title.
TX757.044   1991
641.8'13 — dc20
                                                    91-8674
                                                    CIP

Printed in the United States of America

BOOKS ARE AVAILABLE AT QUANTITY DISCOUNTS WHEN USED TO PROMOTE PRODUCTS OR SERVICES. FOR INFOR-
MATION PLEASE WRITE TO PREMIUM MARKETING DIVISION, PENGUIN BOOKS USA INC. 375 HUDSON STREET,
NEW YORK, NEW YORK 10014

CONTENTS

❧

INTRODUCTION

Soups are integral to life and have been ever since human beings first boiled bones and roots in a fire pot at the family cave. For millennia soups have been made in every culture and, it's safe to say, every home. Some soups are so popular that they're identified with national and regional cultures, and you can match the soup with the group — onion soup, borscht, posole, kale soup, gumbo, shark's fin soup.

Fortunately, regional and international favorites as *French Onion Soup* and *New England Clam Chowder* belong to all of us — no passports needed. In this day and age a wide variety of foods is available. Once-exotic fish and vegetables are commonplace. Most supermarkets feature specialty sections of imported produce and prepared foods. Fish markets display Nova Scotia and Norwegian salmon. Meat counters stock Italian sausage and Danish hams.

As for cooking techniques, soups are easy to prepare. Very few of them require four-star-chef status. This is the democracy of soup making — everyone and anyone can make an aromatic, tasty, healthful, appetizing, and colorful soup.

HOME KITCHEN TESTING

Each recipe in *The Ultimate Soup Book* has been tested by us in our small home kitchen and eaten at our table. As a result, the recipes are designed for ordinary cooks in ordinary kitchens using standard cooking equipment — nothing fancy. In our simple setting we make *Lobster Bisque, Red Sweet Pepper Soup (Chilled), New England Bouillabaisse, Rhubarb Strawberry Soup (Chilled),* and all the rest with minimal effort.

USING THIS BOOK

Since the foundation of soups is the stock, we have grouped the 250 recipes according to the stock used. At your discretion, however, you may wish to interchange stocks. For example, some of the lighter beef-stock-based recipes, such as *Lettuce Soup,* could be made with a vegetable or chicken stock. But we assume that if you like soups you'll want to have basic stocks on hand in the freezer. So grouping according to the stock facilitates finding a suitable recipe. The soups also are cross-referenced by main ingredient in the index.

Each of the five sections of the book begins with basic stocks followed by the recipes calling for those stocks. For example, in the Poultry section, simple recipes for chicken and turkey stocks are given; then 80 recipes using poultry stock follow. The Fruit and Nut section has no stock per se because the fruits and nuts form the soup itself.

Please think of these recipes as suggested guides and not established, rigid laws. No emperor will lop off your head if you use cinnamon instead of allspice or onions instead of shallots. We use a particular combination of ingredients and quantities because they suit us. You may prefer a different combination, and we urge you to follow your creative impulse in the adventure of cooking.

Stocks and Broths

In common parlance the words stock and broth often are interchanged, but we view them as being distinct in nature. To us a stock is the structural foundation of soup — the inconspicuous but vital building block. It has a pivotal position in a recipe. In *The Ultimate Soup Book* the stocks aren't too seasoned for this reason. They support and enhance the conspicuous tastes and flavorings of individual recipes.

A broth includes stock plus a few other ingredients. It is, in fact, an embellished stock served as a soup.

Portions

Most dessert soups, such as *Cranberry Soup (Chilled)* or *Litchi Watermelon Soup (Chilled)*, and the richer cream soups, such as *Scallop Soup, St. Jacques*, are served in smaller portions. But the dinner soups, such as *Guinea Hen, Oyster, and Sausage Gumbo*, are intended to provide a full meal and are served in large bowls. For dinner guests, most of these recipes may be doubled without altering the original desired effect.

Bowls

A clarified consommé fails to show off its shimmering transparency in a peasant-style crude pottery bowl. And *Couscous Soup* loses its earthy character in a dainty Limoges cup. Much of the joy of eating is in the visual presentation of a dish, so select the vessel with care. There is a wide choice:

ovenproof gratin dishes
standard soup bowls
shallow flat soup plates
deep pottery bowls
pottery mugs
Oriental rice bowls
wine or water goblets

glass compotes
punch cups and saucers
marmites (individual casseroles)
double-handled soup cups
soup tureens
china teacups

UTENSILS AND IMPLEMENTS

The kitchen equipment for preparing soups is standard. Most of the utensils probably may be found in your kitchen drawers and cabinets already. Major items include:

blender
cheesecloth and kitchen string
fine mesh strainer
food mill
grater
kitchen shears
measuring cups and spoons
mezza luna or large chopping
   knife
paring knives
saucepans with lids

skillets with lids
slotted spoon
soup ladle
soup or stockpot
steamer
tea ball or teaspoon infuser
   for *bouguet garni*
tongs
vegetable peeler
wok
wooden spoon

INGREDIENTS

The freshness of ingredients plays an essential role in the success of a soup. You have a head start as a soup maker if you're a gardener, too. Those who have harvested corn from their own gardens and cooked it within half an hour before the sugar turns to starch know what we mean. Absolutely fresh produce transforms a ho-hum soup into a dynamic energizer.

Next best to homegrown is to frequent farm stands and stores selling local produce. Then during off-seasons, get to know the produce manager and delivery schedule of your favorite supermarket.

Select vegetables and fruits with discrimination. Check for bruises and discoloration. Is the lettuce perky or brown-edged and droopy? Are the cucumbers narrow and firm? Big soft ones usually have gone to seed. Is the fish bright and glowing or dull and fishy smelling? Is the meat marbled with fat or lean? Touch, taste, sight, and smell all contribute to the selection of the best ingredients. Attentiveness from the initial selection of ingredients to the final seasoning of a soup has an accumulative effect on the end result.

Washing

Always wash vegetables and fruits well in cold water before their preparation. This applies to fish, shellfish, and poultry, too. Leeks notoriously are sandy. The greens of beets, chard, kale, and collards may take two or three thorough washings leaf by leaf. Unfortunately, pesticide and herbicide residues may linger on the surfaces, in the peels, and sometimes in the fruits and vegetables themselves.

Garnishes

The word garnish means "to ornament with something bright and savory." A garnish is a prologue of color, usually sprinkled on top to draw the spoon into the bowl. It's not supposed to upstage a soup but to seduce the diner. Garnishes range from French-fried parsley to slivered almonds and whipped cream. Let your imagination be the guide, and send the bowl to the table with that little extra mint leaf or parsley sprig to trigger the taste buds.

Salt

Most of these soups call for minimal salt. We're convinced that taste enjoyment increases with reduced salt intake. A touch of salt gives verve and depth to a dish, but more than a little masks the subtle nuances of the ingredients.

We prefer sweet butter to salted, not only because we can control the saltiness of the soup but because sweet butter also is usually fresher. (Salt is used in butter as a preservative for longer shelf life.) Also, many foods such as cheese are naturally salty. Today, prepared foods, meats, sausages, wines, and beers are heavily infused with nitrates, nitrites, sodium chloride, and other salts.

VERSATILE SOUP

The universal appeal of soups centers on their adaptability to every occasion. For instance, you can start the day with a *Brazilian Vitamina Soup (Chilled)*, or if you're vacationing and haven't hours to spend in the kitchen you can whip up *Baked Bean Soup*. Celebrating an anniversary or birthday? Pop the cork for an instant salvo of toasts and serve the *Crab Champagne Soup*. Tired of doing the dishes? Prepare a one-pot dinner such as *Kielbasa Cabbage Soup*. Having an elegant dinner party? Kick it off with the *Truffle Soup with Puff Pastry*. Looking for a different but easy dessert? Surprise your family with *Chocolate Mint Soup (Chilled)*. Bored with traditional Thanksgiving dishes? Add *Cranberry Soup (Chilled)* to the menu.

As you can see, soups are extremely versatile. They may be eaten in all seasons for breakfast, brunch, lunch, supper, and dinner. Whether you serve them as appetizers, entrées, or desserts, they are convenient and delicious.

— J.O.
— S.S.

POULTRY

Basic Chicken Stock *3*
Basic Turkey Stock *3*

❧

1

SOUPS

2

꧁

BASIC CHICKEN STOCK

Excess chicken fat may be skimmed off the top if the stock is refrigerated overnight. We prefer to leave some fat in the stock because it lends flavor to the soup. Minimal seasoning is best for all stocks. The seasoning may be added to individual recipes.

4–5 lb stewing chicken
12 C water (enough to cover the chicken)
2 medium-size carrots, chopped

1 large celery stalk (with leaves), chopped
2 parsley sprigs
1 t salt

1. Remove the chicken liver, neck, and other parts usually stored in a bag in the cavity of the chicken.
2. Wash the chicken well inside and out.
3. Place the stewing chicken in a large stockpot with the water and vegetables.
4. Bring the water to a boil. Lower the heat.
5. Cover the stock and let it simmer for 45 minutes.
6. Remove the chicken from the pot. The meat may be used in chicken salad and other dishes.
7. Strain the stock through a double layer of wet cheesecloth placed in a large strainer.
8. Cool the stock thoroughly, and use it in the following recipes. Extra stock may be frozen for 3–4 months in plastic containers. Leave room for expansion in the containers, and be sure to label them with the date and type of stock.

Yields approximately 12 cups

꧁

BASIC TURKEY STOCK

This recipe is meant to make complete use of a holiday turkey. Larger turkeys will require more water to cover the carcass. Keep in mind that you want the stock fairly strong.

Carcass of a 10–14 lb roasted turkey (or whole packaged turkey backs)
10–12 C water (to cover)

1 carrot, chopped
1 large celery stalk (with leaves), chopped
2 parsley sprigs
1 t salt

1. Remove the legs, thighs, wings, and all the stuffing from the carcass. Carve off the meat. You may have to crack the carcass to get it into the pot. Add the wings and leftover skin scraps to the pot.
2. Place the turkey carcass (or whole backs) in a stockpot with the water and the vegetables and bring to a boil. Add salt.
3. Lower the heat, cover, and simmer the stock for 1 hour.
4. Remove the turkey parts and discard them.
5. Strain the stock through a double layer of wet cheesecloth placed in a large strainer.
6. Cool the stock thoroughly.
7. You can store the stock 3–4 months in plastic containers in a freezer compartment.

Yields approximately 10–12 cups

֍

ARTICHOKE SOUP

This soup has a delicate, unusual flavor and makes an elegant appetizer. The frozen hearts are less trouble, but fresh artichokes produce a more tantalizing flavor. Either way, this is a singular soup.

3 T sweet butter
¼ C flour
1½ C milk
2 C artichoke hearts (4 large, fresh artichokes or two 9-oz packages, frozen)

3 C chicken stock
¼ t nutmeg
½ t lemon juice
Salt
Sprinkle of white pepper

1. Make a white sauce: melt 2 tablespoons butter and add the flour. Stirring constantly with a whisk, add the milk. Cook over medium-low heat for 7–10 minutes until the sauce is very thick.
2. Sauté the artichoke hearts in 1 tablespoon butter. (Note: if hearts are frozen, cook according to package directions first. If using fresh artichokes, boil them until they are easily punctured with a fork. Cut them into quarters and remove the hairy choke center. Remove the thorny tips of leaves by cutting off the tops. Leave the tender leaves on the hearts and slice them.)
3. Work the artichoke hearts through the medium disc of a food mill.
4. Add the ground artichoke hearts and chicken stock to the white sauce, and heat the mixture over low heat.
5. Season the soup with nutmeg, lemon juice, salt, and pepper to taste.

Serves 5–7

ॐ

Avgolemono Soup

Avgolemono or egg lemon soup is a favorite Greek specialty prepared in most Greek restaurants and homes—and for good reason. Be sure to use the juice from a fresh lemon. It adds an important difference to the taste.

6 C chicken stock
⅓ C white rice

2 large eggs
¼ C fresh lemon juice
½ t salt

1. Bring the stock to a boil in a large saucepan.
2. Add the rice, cover, and simmer over low heat for 20 minutes.
3. In a large mixing bowl, beat the eggs. (Another egg may be added for a thicker soup.)
4. Whip the lemon juice into the eggs.
5. Constantly whip the lemon-egg mixture while you add 2 cups of the hot stock. (The stock will pour off the top and most of the rice will remain at the bottom of the saucepan.)
6. Just before serving, add the egg-lemon-stock mixture to the rest of the rice and chicken stock, whisking constantly while heating the soup over a medium-low burner. Do not boil the soup or the eggs will coagulate.
7. Add the salt.
8. Let the soup stand covered off the burner for 5 minutes.

Serves 4–6

ℰ
AVOCADO SOUP (CHILLED)

At most, chilled avocado soup takes 3 minutes to prepare, and its original flavor is sure to spark favorable comment.

1 ½ C avocado pulp
2 ½ C chicken stock (more for a
    thinner consistency)

2 t lemon juice
⅛ t Tabasco sauce
1 t grated onion
Salt

1. Halve the avocado(s) and scoop out the pulp.
2. Place all the ingredients with the avocado in a blender. Purée well.
3. Chill the soup thoroughly in the blender container.
4. Serve in chilled white or clear glass bowls.

Serves 4

ℰ
BARLEY AND BULGUR SOUP (CHILLED)

Add more yogurt if you prefer a lighter soup. This is a peasant soup with the flavor of the Russian steppes to it — hearty and healthy.

2 T olive oil
½ C onion, peeled and diced
2 C chicken stock
2 T pearl barley

2 T bulgur wheat
2 C plain yogurt
1 T strong mint tea, cooled to
    room temperature

1. Heat the oil in a large saucepan over medium-low heat. Stir in the onion, cover, and sweat them for 5–8 minutes or until golden.
2. Add the chicken stock and bring it to a boil.
3. Stir in the barley. Cover and simmer the soup for 30 minutes over medium-low heat.
4. Stir in the bulgur wheat. Cover and continue cooking the soup at a low boil for 20 minutes more or until the wheat is soft.
5. Cool the soup at room temperature.
6. Stir in the yogurt and tea, and refrigerate at least an hour before serving.

Serves 4

BEER SOUP

Beer soups are popular in Europe, and this one is particularly mild because it uses a light-colored and -flavored lager.

2 T sweet butter	Salt
⅓ C onion, peeled and minced	Sprinkle of white pepper
1 garlic clove, peeled and minced	Sprinkle of freshly grated nut-
5 C chicken stock	meg
1 C lager beer	¼ C heavy cream
1 C fine white bread crumbs	1 T parsley, de-stemmed and
	minced

1. Melt the butter in a heavy skillet over low heat.
2. Add the onion and garlic. Cover and let them sweat 5–8 minutes.
3. In a medium-size soup pot, combine the chicken stock with the beer.
4. Add the bread crumbs and cooked onion and garlic to the stock.
5. Taste the soup to see if salt is needed.
6. Add the pepper and nutmeg.
7. Cover the soup and simmer it for 30 minutes.
8. Add the cream immediately before serving. Reheat but don't boil the soup.
9. Garnish each bowl with a sprinkle of parsley.

Serves 5–6

ও

BLACK BEAN SOUP

The piquancy of this classic Mexican soup is adjusted easily by the amount of jalapeño seeds. One or 2 seeds along with the green flesh is about right for most people. These peppers are like little bombs. They don't register on the supermarket scales, but they do register on the palate!

1 C black beans (water to cover)	½ C onion, peeled and diced
4 C water	1 small green jalapeño chile,
⅛ lb salt pork, blanched	de-seeded of all but 2–3 seeds
2 C chicken stock	(wear gloves) and minced
1 ripe tomato, diced	½ t oregano
½ t salt	1 ½ T olive oil
2 garlic cloves, peeled and	2 T dry sherry
minced	Sour cream

1. Wash the beans and place them in a heavy saucepan. Add water to cover them, and bring it to a boil over high heat. Boil the beans for 10 minutes. Cover the beans, and remove the saucepan from the burner. Let the beans stand for 1 hour. (This process helps to soften dry beans and shortens the cooking time.)
2. Measure the water left in the beans and add enough to equal 4 cups.
3. Add the salt pork, chicken stock, tomato, and salt, and bring to a boil. Reduce the heat and simmer the beans for 1½–2 hours.
4. Meanwhile, in a skillet over medium heat, sauté the garlic, onion, jalapeño chile, and oregano in the olive oil.
5. Add this mixture to the beans.
6. When the beans are tender (try one to see), purée them with the soup liquid in a blender. If the purée seems too thick, some water or stock may be added. If it seems too thin, some of the soup liquid may be left out.
7. Return the purée to the pot and stir in the sherry.
8. Reheat the soup just to boiling. Serve each bowlful with a dollop of sour cream.

Serves 4

&ℭ

Broccoli Tahini Soup

Sesame tahini is a paste made of ground hulled sesame seeds. It is found in most health food stores. The sesame oil tends to separate from the paste, so stir the tahini paste well before using it.

2 C broccoli flowers	**1 C water**
Water to cover	**3 T sesame tahini paste**
2 T lemon juice	**1 t lemon juice**
3 C chicken stock	**Salt**

1. Cut the broccoli flowers from the stems, place in a bowl, and cover with water. Add 2 tablespoons of lemon juice. Weight down the flowers with a saucer. Soak 15 minutes.
2. Drain the broccoli, and place it in a saucepan with the chicken stock and 1 cup water.
3. Bring the stock and water to a boil. Lower the heat, cover, and simmer the flowers until they are bright green and tender.
4. Pour off 2 cups of the liquid. Cool it (5–8 minutes) and place it in a blender with the tahini paste. The liquid must be cool or the paste will curdle.

5. Blend the tahini and liquid well.
6. Pour this mixture back into the saucepan with the broccoli.
7. Add 1 teaspoon lemon juice and salt to taste.
8. Reheat but do not boil the soup.

Serves 4

৵

BUTTERNUT BISQUE

Velvety and golden. If the bisque seems too thick, thin it with a light touch of extra stock or cream.

1 T olive oil
1 T sweet butter
⅓ C onion, peeled and chopped
1⅔ C chicken stock
½ C carrots, diced

3 C butternut squash, peeled, seeded, and chopped
½ t salt
Sprinkle of white pepper
Freshly grated nutmeg
⅓ C heavy cream

1. In a large saucepan, heat the oil and butter. Add the onion and sauté 3–4 minutes over medium-low heat.
2. Add the stock, carrots, and squash. Boil the vegetables for 30 minutes over medium heat.
3. Pour the vegetables and stock in a blender and purée. Return the purée to the rinsed saucepan.
4. Add the salt, white pepper, and nutmeg to taste.
5. Add the cream. Reheat but do not boil the soup before serving.

Serves 4

POULTRY

9

æ

CALIFORNIA BLACK OLIVE SOUP

The texture of black olives resembles that of mushrooms. This West Coast specialty makes an intriguing appetizer or light luncheon soup.

1 T olive oil
2 T onion, peeled and diced
1 small garlic clove, peeled, crushed, and minced
1 T parsley, de-stemmed and minced

2 C chicken stock
½ C pitted California black olives, minced
1 egg yolk
½ C heavy cream (approximately)

1. Heat the oil in a large saucepan over medium-low heat. Sauté the onion, garlic, and parsley briefly. Cover and let them sweat for 5–8 minutes, stirring occasionally to avoid browning.
2. Add the chicken stock and olives. Bring them to a simmer and cook for 10 minutes.
3. Place the egg yolk in a measuring cup, and add enough cream to make ½ cup. Pour into a small bowl and blend with a whisk.
4. Remove ¼ cup of the olive mixture, and slowly whisk it into the cream-egg mixture. Pour this liaison back into the soup.
5. Bring the soup to the simmering point, stirring well for 5 minutes as the soup thickens. Do not boil.

Serves 4

æ

CARROT APPLE SOUP (CHILLED)

The combination of fruits with vegetables is overlooked too often. This soup joins carrots and apples so well that their taste is inseparable.

3 T sweet butter
2 leeks (white part only), thinly sliced
⅛ t marjoram
⅛ t thyme
5 C chicken stock

3 C carrots, scraped and diced
2 C Granny Smith apples, peeled, cored, and diced
Salt
½ C half-and-half
Freshly grated nutmeg

1. Melt the butter in a large soup pot over low heat, and sauté the leeks in the butter with the marjoram and thyme.
2. Cover the leeks and sweat them for 5–8 minutes or until soft.

3. Add the chicken stock, carrots, apples, and salt, if needed.
4. Bring the soup to a boil over high heat. Lower the heat, cover the pot, and simmer the soup for 35 minutes.
5. Cool the soup to room temperature and refrigerate it overnight.
6. Skim the chicken fat and butter from the top of the soup and reserve it for other uses. Blend the soup in a blender for 2 minutes.
7. Transfer the soup to a food mill. Using the finest disc, pass the soup through the mill into a bowl, adding the half-and-half. Chill completely before serving.
8. Grate fresh nutmeg onto each portion.

Serves 4

&

CARROT ORANGE SOUP

This is a perky carrot soup with a lively, edgy taste to match its deep orange color. It's an easy one-pot soup for hurried days.

2 T olive oil	2 C carrots, scraped and diced
¼ C onion, peeled and diced	1 T fresh mint leaves, minced
2 C chicken stock	½ t salt
1 t grated orange rind	Sour cream
⅓ C fresh orange juice	Chives, minced

1. In a large saucepan, heat the oil and sauté the onion. Cover and sweat 5–8 minutes over medium-low heat.
2. Add the chicken stock, orange rind and juice, carrots, and mint. Bring the soup to a boil, cover, and simmer it for 25–30 minutes or until the carrots are soft. Cool.
3. Pour the soup into a blender, and purée it for 1 minute.
4. Return the soup to the rinsed saucepan, add salt, and reheat. Serve with a dollop of sour cream and a sprinkle of chives.

Serves 4

CELERIAC SOUP

Celeriac looks like a large turnip but tastes vaguely like celery. It has a subtle, sweet taste and makes an elegant and irresistible soup served either chilled or hot.

3 T sweet butter
1 C leeks (white part only),
   thinly sliced
Pinch of thyme
Sprinkle of white pepper

1½ lb celeriac (about 4 C),
   peeled and diced
1 C potatoes, peeled and diced
5½ C turkey or chicken stock
½ C heavy cream
Parsley, de-stemmed and minced

1. In a large skillet, melt the butter over medium heat and sauté the leeks a few minutes. Add the thyme and white pepper. Turn the heat to low, cover the skillet, and sweat the leeks 2–3 minutes.
2. Peel and dice the celeriac. Add the potatoes and celeriac to the skillet. Stir, cover, and cook them about 10 minutes over medium-low heat, stirring occasionally. Don't let the mixture brown.
3. Heat the stock in a large soup pot. Add the vegetables, and bring the soup to a boil. Reduce the heat to medium. Cover and simmer the stock and vegetables for 20 minutes.
4. With a slotted spoon, place half the vegetables in a blender and pour in half the liquid. Blend it until smooth, and pour the purée into a bowl. Repeat with the second half.
5. Pour all of the blended soup back into the soup pot. Add the cream and heat the soup thoroughly. Taste and correct for salt. Sprinkle parsley on each portion as a garnish.

Serves 6

SOUPS

12

CHESTNUT SOUP

The chestnut purée freezes well and may be used for future soups or, mixed with sugar, in toppings for coffee cakes and rolls.

1 ½ lb chestnuts
1 T vegetable oil
Bouquet garni (see right)
Hot water
½ t salt
5 C chicken stock
Sprinkle of white pepper
Sprinkle of paprika
1 C heavy cream
⅛ t dry mustard
Salt

3 T sherry
½ t sugar
Sprinkle of ground walnuts

BOUQUET GARNI
3 celery leaf sprigs
4 parsley sprigs
1 small piece bay leaf
⅛ t dried thyme (or 1 fresh
   sprig)
1 clove

1. Using a sharp paring knife, score the rounded part of each chestnut with a crisscross. Wear gloves and be careful; the shell is tough.
2. Preheat the oven to 450° F.
3. Place the oil in a large, 10-inch iron skillet or any other shallow oven-proof receptacle with a handle.
4. Add the chestnuts to the skillet and place it in the oven.
5. Shake the chestnuts occasionally, remembering to use a pot holder. In 10–15 minutes the chestnuts will burst open and sizzle. Take them out and cool them just long enough so that you can handle them. Remember to use a pot holder when you remove them from the oven as well. Peel them with a knife, removing the outer and inner skins.
6. Make the bouquet garni by placing ingredients listed under bouquet garni in a small square of cheesecloth and tying off with kitchen thread. Alternately, ingredients may be placed in a tea infuser.
7. Place the chestnuts in a medium-size saucepan. Cover them with hot water and add ½ teaspoon of salt and the bouquet garni.
8. Bring the chestnuts to a boil. Lower the heat to medium, cover the pan, and simmer them at a low boil for 25 minutes. The chestnuts should be soft.
9. Discard the bouquet garni and drain the chestnuts.
10. Using the finest disc of a food mill, grind the chestnuts into a bowl. This will take muscle, unless you use a cup or so of chicken stock to ease the chestnuts through.
11. There should be about 3–4 cups of chestnut purée.
12. Place the remaining chicken stock in a soup pot. Add the purée to the stock along with the white pepper and paprika.

13. Heat the soup over medium-low heat until it has boiled once. Remove it from the heat and stir in ½ cup cream and the dry mustard. Add salt to taste and the sherry. Whip the remaining ½ cup cream with the sugar. Serve chestnut soup in mugs with a dollop of whipped cream sprinkled with the walnuts.

Serves 6

ৱ

CHICKEN CHILE SOUP

This Mexican-style soup is mildly piquant and can be whipped up in short order. Be sure to wear rubber gloves when working with chiles, and keep your hands away from your face when you handle them. Nachos are a good accompaniment for this delicious olé *soup.*

2 T olive oil
½ C onion, peeled and diced
½ C yellow wax or Anaheim chiles (2–3 of them), cored, de-seeded, and diced
1 T jalapeño chile (1 small chile), de-seeded except for 2–3 seeds, and minced
2 C chicken stock
1 C tomatoes, peeled and chopped, with juice

3 T parsley, de-stemmed and minced
¼ C fresh lime juice
1 t grated lime rind
½ t cumin
½ t salt
Freshly ground black pepper
1 C cooked shredded chicken breast (deboned and skinned; these may be used for stock)
1 C avocado, de-seeded, peeled, and chopped

1. In a large saucepan heat the oil over medium-high heat. Add the onion and the 2 chiles. Sauté them briefly. Cover the pan and let the vegetables sweat for 5–8 minutes over medium-low heat.
2. Add the chicken stock, tomatoes, parsley, lime juice and rind, cumin, salt, and pepper.
3. Cover the soup and simmer it for 15 minutes.
4. Immediately before serving, add the shredded chicken and avocado.
5. Heat the soup but do not let it boil.

Serves 4

CHICKEN GUMBO

Gumbo is a southern Creole dish. Many recipes call for filé powder, which is a thickening agent made from sassafras. The powder is now banned as a carcinogen. If you like extra thick soup, 1 tablespoon of arrowroot or 2 tablespoons of cornstarch may be mixed with a little water and stirred into the soup. However, we've found that the okra thickens the soup sufficiently without additional starches.

3 rashers bacon, diced
2 chicken breasts, split
Flour
4 C water
4 C 1-inch pieces okra (or 2 10-oz frozen packages)
½ C sweet green pepper, cored, de-seeded, and diced
⅓ C onion, peeled and diced
1 T parsley, de-stemmed and minced

2 C whole tomatoes, peeled, with juice
⅓ C tomato paste
½ lb cured cooked ham steak
¼ lb shrimp, cooked, de-veined, and peeled
Salt
½ t Tabasco sauce
Cooked rice (optional)

1. Fry the bacon in a large skillet. Pour off half the drippings with the bacon pieces, and retain half the fat in the pan.
2. Dredge the 4 chicken pieces in the flour, and fry them in the bacon fat until they're brown.
3. Cover the chicken with the water, and cook at a low boil for 20 minutes.
4. In a large soup pot sauté all the vegetables except the tomatoes in the remaining bacon fat with the bacon bits for 10 minutes.
5. Add the tomatoes and tomato paste.
6. Drain the chicken, and pour the stock into the soup pot with the vegetables.
7. Remove the chicken from the bones, and tear it into bite-size shreds.
8. Dice the ham and cut the shrimp into bite-size pieces.
9. Add the ham, shrimp, and chicken to the soup pot.
10. Bring the gumbo to a boil, lower the heat, and simmer, covered, for 1 hour.
11. Salt to taste and add the hot sauce last.
12. Pass around a bowl of rice or place a scoop of rice in each bowl.

Serves 6–8

CHICKEN LEG NOODLE SOUP

Chicken soup is proverbial. If it did everything it was supposed to, the soup would replace the medical profession. Mystique aside, chicken soup is a comforting, homey dish and standard repertoire for all generations.

4 chicken legs (with thighs)
10 C water
1 large celery stalk with leaves,
   cut in half

Salt
2 C thin egg noodles

1. In a large soup pot, cover the legs with water (allow 2 ½ cups water for each chicken leg and 1 leg per person). Add the celery.
2. Bring the water to a boil. Reduce the heat to a low boil. Cover and simmer 1 hour.
3. Salt the stock to taste.
4. Remove the legs and celery. Pick the meat from the legs, discarding the skin and bones.
5. Add the chicken meat to the stock. Bring it to a boil and add the noodles.
6. Reduce the heat to medium and boil the soup, uncovered, 7–10 minutes, or until the noodles are soft but firm—al dente.

Serves 4

CHICKEN SUBGUM SOUP

Subgum refers to a festive, colorful dish with many ingredients. You can buy a split chicken breast, debone it, skin it, and make the stock from these chicken parts, reserving the fresh meat for the soup.

3 T safflower oil
½ C Chinese celery
2 scallions, white part plus 2
   inches of the green stalk, diced
1 chicken breast, deboned,
   skinned, and cut into strips
8 snow peas, ends removed and
   sliced diagonally

¼ C water chestnuts, rinsed,
   drained, and diced
1 T sweet red pepper, diced
½ C mung bean sprouts
3 C chicken stock
Salt
1 T cornstarch
½ C water
1 egg, beaten

1. Place the oil in a wok over medium-high heat.
2. Add the celery, scallions, chicken, and snow peas.
3. Stir-fry the vegetables 3 minutes.
4. Add the water chestnuts, sweet red pepper, and bean sprouts.
5. Stir-fry another minute.
6. Add the chicken stock to the wok, and bring the soup to a boil over high heat. Add salt to taste.
7. Mix the cornstarch with the water, add this mixture to the soup, and simmer the soup until it clears (about 2 minutes).
8. Slowly whisk in the egg as you pour it in a slow stream into the broth to form threads. Serve immediately.

Serves 4

POULTRY
17

CHICKEN WITH MATZO BALL SOUP

Matzo balls are filling and delectable with the slight crunch of sesame seeds. The stock should be rich and flavorful for ultimate satisfaction.

2 extra large eggs, slightly beaten
2 T chicken fat or vegetable
  shortening
½ C matzo meal
½ t salt
2 T water
1 T toasted sesame seeds

2 T parsley, de-stemmed and
  minced
8 C water
4 – 5 C chicken stock
Pinch of sage
Salt

1. In a medium bowl stir together the eggs and fat (or shortening).
2. With a wooden spoon, mix the matzo meal and salt into the egg mixture.
3. Stir in the 2 tablespoons water, toasted sesame seeds, and parsley. (To toast the seeds, simply place them in a dry frying pan over low heat. Shake the seeds in the pan until they turn golden in color and are starting to pop.)
4. Cover the bowl, and refrigerate the dough for 15 – 20 minutes until it is chilled enough to form firm balls.
5. Remove the dough, and by hand form the balls about 1 inch in diameter.
6. Bring about 8 cups of water to a boil in a large pot with a lid.
7. Gently add the matzo balls. Cover the pot, and reduce the heat so the matzo balls simmer at a low boil for about 20 – 30 minutes. The balls will float and double in size when they're ready.
8. Meanwhile, heat the stock in a fairly large saucepan so that the stock is simmering when the matzo balls are ready. Add the sage and taste for salt.
9. Drain the matzo balls, and add them to the stock. Serve a few balls in each bowl of soup.

Serves 4

SOUPS

18

CHICK-PEA SOUP

This soup is simple and healthy. Chick-peas, or garbanzos, may be found in the import or specialty section of your supermarket.

3½ C cooked prepared chick-
   peas, skins removed
6 C water
2 C chicken stock
½ C onion, peeled and diced
1 large ripe tomato, peeled and
   cored
1 bay leaf
1 t parsley, de-stemmed and
   minced

3 garlic cloves, peeled, crushed,
   and minced
⅛ t hot red chile sauce
1 T olive oil
1 lb fresh spinach, de-stemmed
   and cut in thin strips (chiffonade)
2 t wine vinegar
Salt

1. Wash and drain the prepared chick-peas. Remove the skins by hand.
2. Mix the water and chicken stock in a large soup pot and bring it to a boil.
3. Add 1 ½ cups chick-peas, onion, tomato, bay leaf, parsley, garlic cloves, and the chile sauce.
4. Lower the heat so the soup cooks at a low boil and simmer, covered, for 45 minutes.
5. Strain the vegetables from the stock. Return the stock to the rinsed pan. Discard the bay leaf. Purée the vegetables with the olive oil through a fine disc of a food mill or in a blender.
6. Return the chick-pea mixture to the stock and stir it in.
7. Add the spinach and cook another 15 minutes.
8. Add the remaining 2 cups of whole chick-peas and the vinegar last. Salt to taste.

Serves 6–8

POULTRY

19

꿍

CREAM OF TURKEY SOUP

This soup is a cousin to Turkey à la King. Accompany it with a basket of hot crumbly biscuits and cranberry relish for a postholiday lunch or supper.

2 C turkey stock	1 C turkey (white meat only), cut
2 C milk	in bite-size pieces
3 T flour	Salt
½ C pimento-stuffed olives,	Sprinkle of white pepper
chopped	2 T almonds, blanched, peeled,
	and slivered

1. Place the turkey stock and 1 ½ cups of the milk in a soup pot. Heat to the simmering point.
2. Place the flour in a small mixing bowl, and blend in the remaining ½ cup of milk to form a paste.
3. Add the flour mixture to the soup. Heat and stir with a whisk 5–7 minutes or until the soup thickens.
4. Add the olives and turkey.
5. Taste for seasoning. (Olives are salty so be sure to taste the soup before adding salt.)
6. Serve each portion with a garnish of almonds.

Serves 4

꿍

CREAMY BUTTER BEAN SOUP

Nutritious, large, yellow lima beans are called butter beans, which form the foundation for this quick-to-make soup. You can easily double and triple this recipe for guests.

2 rashers lean bacon, diced	1 can butter beans (15 oz),
1 t olive oil	drained
1 C tomatoes, peeled, with juice	2 C chicken stock
1 T grated onion	

1. Over medium heat sauté the bacon in the olive oil in a medium-size skillet.
2. Pass the tomatoes through a food mill or strainer to extract the seeds.
3. If there is more than 1 teaspoon of fat rendered from the bacon, pour it off.

4. Add the grated onion to the fat and lower the heat to medium-low. Sauté the onion 2–3 minutes.
5. Add the tomatoes, and simmer them while preparing the butter beans.
6. Remove and discard any loose skins from the beans. The skins are tough and will not blend easily.
7. Place the beans and 1 cup of chicken stock in a blender and blend them for 2 minutes.
8. Add the onion-tomato-bacon mixture, and continue to blend them for 2 minutes.
9. Place the blended mixture in a medium-size soup pot, and heat the soup over medium heat. Add the remaining cup of chicken stock, stir, and heat the soup until it reaches the boiling point.

Serves 4

&

CUCUMBER SOUP (CHILLED)

This exquisite summer soup enhances a brunch, light elegant lunch, or high tea. A simple garden salad of Bibb lettuce and tomatoes adds a nuance of color to the meal.

½ C shallots, peeled and diced
3 T sweet butter
3 ½ C cucumber, peeled, seeded, and cut into ½ -inch pieces
6 C chicken stock
2 t wine vinegar

1 t dried dill
Salt
Sprinkle of white pepper
½ C sour cream
Mint leaves (optional)

1. In a skillet sauté the shallots in the butter until golden and soft, 5–8 minutes over low heat.
2. Add the cucumber, stock, vinegar, and dill.
3. Simmer the soup, covered, for 30 minutes until the cucumber is soft.
4. Purée the soup in a blender.
5. Add the salt and white pepper to taste.
6. Whisk the sour cream into the warm soup.
7. Refrigerate the soup for at least 3 hours.
8. Pour the soup into chilled bowls, and serve it with a sprig of mint floating in the center of each bowl.

Serves 4–6

DRY SOUP

Sopa seca *or dry soup is an amusing contradiction in terms. Mexicans prepare* sopa seca *out of anything—noodles, tortillas, bread. South of the border, stale tortillas are the handiest common denominator.*

¼ C corn oil
6 oz thin egg noodles or vermicelli broken into 2-inch pieces
¼ C onion, peeled and diced
2 garlic cloves, peeled, crushed, and minced
2 C whole tomatoes, peeled, with juice

1 t jalapeño pepper sauce (salsa)
1 C chicken stock
¼ t oregano
Salt
Freshly ground black pepper
Monterey Jack cheese

1. Place the oil in a large skillet over medium heat.
2. Sauté the noodles until they're golden brown.
3. Remove the noodles with a slotted spoon, leaving as much oil in the skillet as possible.
4. Sauté the onion and garlic in the remaining oil for 5 minutes.
5. Add the tomatoes, jalapeño sauce, noodles, and chicken stock. Cover with a tight lid.
6. Cook the soup over low heat until it is nearly dry (about 30 minutes). Stir in the salt and pepper to taste.
7. Serve the dry soup with grated cheese.

Serves 4

SOUPS

DUCK GUMBO

Originally, wild duck from the bayous of Louisiana was the basic ingredient for duck gumbo, a Cajun specialty. Gombo *is the African Congolese name of the seed pod of okra.*

2 ducks (4½–5 lbs each), trimmed of excess fatty skin
Water to cover ducks
¼ lb bacon, sliced and diced
4 T bacon fat, rendered from the bacon
3 T flour
½ C scallions (white part only), thinly sliced
½ C celery, threaded and diced
¼ C sweet green bell pepper, cored, seeded, and diced

1½ C okra, trimmed and sliced into ½-inch pieces
1 garlic clove, peeled, crushed, and minced
2 C degreased duck stock
4 C chicken stock
1 t chile powder
1 t Tabasco sauce
1 T Worcestershire sauce
Salt
Cooked rice (½ C per serving)
2 T parsley, de-stemmed and minced

1. Place each duck in its own large pot. Cover each duck with water and boil over high heat. Lower the heat to a simmer and cover the ducks. Cook them 1 hour.
2. Remove the ducks, and place them in a shallow roasting pan to cool to room temperature; then refrigerate. Pour the stock from the ducks into a bowl and also refrigerate. Do this a day ahead so the grease will solidify for removal. Degrease the stock before using it. Pour off 2 cups of the duck stock for the gumbo, and freeze the remaining stock for other recipes. (Duck stock is very rich and should be used in moderation or diluted with water.)
3. Remove the skin and bones from the duck meat, quite a messy job. Shred the duck meat into bite-size pieces.
4. Fry the bacon in a heavy skillet over medium heat until 4 tablespoons of bacon fat have been rendered. Remove the crisp bacon with a slotted spoon and reserve. Pour off any excess fat.
5. Add the flour to the bacon fat, making a roux. Whisk the roux constantly, with the burner on medium-low heat, until it turns smooth and chocolate colored. This roux will take about 2 minutes to brown under constant surveillance and whisking.
6. Add the scallions, celery, sweet green pepper, okra, and garlic to the roux. Sauté the vegetables in the roux for 2 minutes until they are completely coated.
7. Place the 2 cups of duck stock with the chicken stock in a large Dutch

oven or soup pot. Add the sautéed vegetables, cleaning out the skillet with a little stock to get all of the roux into the soup pot.

8. Season the gumbo with chile powder, Tabasco, and Worcestershire sauce. Adjust for salt. If the stocks are salted, the gumbo shouldn't need additional salt.
9. Cover and simmer the gumbo for 40 minutes over medium heat.
10. Add the duck meat and bacon pieces. Simmer the gumbo another 10 minutes.
11. Serve gumbo over rice with a parsley garnish.

Serves 6

ॐ

DUCK SOUP

This soup is extravagant in ingredients but turns out not half as rich as some cream soups. It makes an elegant light supper for guests. Use only fine burgundy, and try to make the soup when fresh apple cider is in season.

1 4 – 5 lb duck cut into pieces and trimmed of excess fat
½ C wild rice
Bouquet garni (see right)
2 C apple cider
4 C burgundy wine
4 C water
1 T arrowroot
½ C cold water
Pinch of mace
Salt

Freshly ground black pepper
1 jigger hard cider (if not available, a jigger of brandy, jigger of beer, or both mixed)

BOUQUET GARNI

3 shallots (peeled)
3 parsley sprigs
1 bay leaf
½ t marjoram
½ t sage leaves
3 peppercorns

1. In a large pot place the duck on top of the rice. Add the bouquet garni and cover the duck with the cider and burgundy.
2. Bring to a boil. Reduce the heat to a low boil, cover, and simmer for 2 hours.
3. With a slotted spoon transfer the pieces of duck to a bowl. Cool.
4. Strain out the rice, removing the bouquet garni. Run water through the rice to rinse off any fat.
5. The stock will have a layer of fat. To make skimming easier, place the stock in a freezer compartment. It will set in approximately 30 minutes. Skim the solidified fat off the top of the stock, and return the stock to the soup pot.

6. After the duck has cooled, pick all meat off the bones, and cut or shred it into small bite-size pieces.
7. Add the rice and duck meat to the soup along with 4 cups of water. Boil it gently another 15 minutes to blend the flavors.
8. Dissolve the arrowroot in ½ cup cold water. Add this mixture to the soup, and stir it while continuing to heat the soup another 5 minutes.
9. Taste. Season with mace, salt, and pepper.
10. Add the hard cider (applejack). Serve the soup in large shallow soup bowls.

Serves 6

ॐ

FRIED PLANTAIN SOUP

Plantains resemble bananas but are a chartreuse color when they ripen. Peel them well; the integument is bitter. Always cook plantains, and always stir the soup when heating it; the plantain starch tends to coagulate on the bottom of the pan.

4 ½ C chicken or turkey stock   **Safflower oil**
2 C plantains (2 whole plantains)   **½ t salt**
Salted water to cover   **Grated Monterey Jack cheese**

1. Heat the chicken stock in a large saucepan placed over medium heat.
2. Peel the plantains under running water. Slice them into ½-inch rounds, and soak them in warm, salted water to cover for 10 minutes.
3. Drain the slices, and place them on paper towels. Make sure the slices are thoroughly dry.
4. Deep-fry the plantains in safflower oil in a deep fryer. The oil should reach 350° F. (A wok works well for deep frying and takes less oil.)
5. When the slices turn from pink to a golden color, remove them and drain on paper towels.
6. Place 2 cups of the stock with the plantains in a blender and blend until creamy. Add the salt and remaining stock and blend another minute.
7. Heat the soup and serve it with a spoonful of cheese garnish on each serving.

Serves 4

Fromage de Chevre Soup

A creamy, not crumbly, goat cheese is a must for this soup. Try the Italian Latte di Capra, Caprini di Capra, or the French Buchette. This soup has a stimulating flavor that whets the appetite for more. It may be served hot or chilled.

¾ lb string beans, de-stemmed
   and snapped into pieces
Water
2 C chicken stock

2 T sweet butter
¼ C onion, peeled and diced
½ lb cream-style goat cheese

1. Steam the string beans in a vegetable steamer over boiling water, covered, for 20 minutes.
2. Place the chicken stock and steamed string beans in a blender, and purée them for 1 minute. Pour the purée into a medium-size saucepan.
3. Melt the butter in a small saucepan. Add the onion and sauté over medium heat for 2–3 minutes. Cover the onion, lower the heat, and sweat until golden (5–8 minutes).
4. Purée the onion in the blender with some of the string bean purée. Add the onion mixture to the rest of the bean purée.
5. Heat the soup to just below boiling.
6. Cut the creamy goat cheese into small slices. Add them to the string bean mixture, and whisk the soup as the cheese melts.
7. When the cheese is completely melted, the soup is ready to serve.

Serves 4

Garlic Soup

Because of the way the garlic blends with the other flavors, you'll never know this is garlic soup unless you make it yourself. In fact, for a meal that's memorable try this soup with French bread and fine French wine and cheese.

3 T olive oil
1 C French bread, cut into croutons and left out overnight
2 large garlic cloves, peeled
1 t paprika
⅛ t cayenne

5 C stock (half chicken, half
   beef)
2 eggs, slightly beaten
2 T parsley, de-stemmed and
   minced
Salt

1. Heat the olive oil in a large heavy saucepan over medium-high heat.
2. Add the croutons and brown them in the oil. When almost brown, press the garlic with the side of a knife, mince, and add to the pan.
3. Sauté the garlic and croutons approximately 3 more minutes.
4. Remove ¾ of the croutons and reserve them.
5. Add paprika, cayenne, and stock to those croutons left in the pan.
6. Bring the soup to a boil.
7. Remove the pan from the heat, and then quickly add the eggs, parsley, and salt to taste while stirring constantly.
8. Cover the soup and let it stand for 5 minutes.
9. Warm the bowls with hot water. Pour out the water and ladle the soup into the bowls. Serve a few saturated croutons in each bowl, and let guests help themselves to the reserved crisp croutons at the table.

Serves 4

ɞ
GREEN CHILE SOUP

The chiles in this recipe are mild, but a slight sizzle does occur on the lips and throat. Smallish servings are better. People who like to play with fire can always ask for more.

2 T sweet butter
½ C onion, peeled and minced
¼ t cumin
6 oz cream cheese

1 C prepared mild green chiles,
** drained and chopped**
1 ¼ C chicken stock

1. Melt the butter in a medium-size saucepan over low heat.
2. Add the onion and cumin.
3. Cover and sweat the onion 5–8 minutes until golden.
4. In a blender, blend the cream cheese and chiles until they are smooth.
5. Add the onion and process the mixture well for 2–3 minutes.
6. Place the chile mixture in a saucepan with the chicken stock and heat, but don't boil the soup.

Serves 4

꙳

GUINEA HEN, OYSTER, AND
SAUSAGE GUMBO

This soup provides a fish-fowl-meat dinner in one pot. As with most New Orleans dishes, make sure a bowl of rice and the Tabasco sauce are on the table.

4 T safflower oil
½ C onion, peeled and diced
¼ C parsley, de-stemmed and minced
¾ C okra, ends trimmed, cut in ½ -inch rounds (about 10 pods)
2 guinea hens

½ lb chorizo (or other hot sausage), cut in bite-size pieces
1½ T flour
½ C dry white vermouth
1 C tomatoes, peeled, with juice
4 C water
8 oysters, shucked, with liqueur
Tabasco sauce

1. Place 2 tablespoons of oil in a large Dutch oven over medium heat, and sauté the onion, parsley, and okra. Cover and let the vegetables sweat for 5 minutes.
2. Remove the vegetables with a slotted spoon and reserve.
3. Remove the liver and other parts stored inside the cavity of each hen. Cut the guinea hens in half with poultry shears. Wash and pat them dry with paper towels. In the Dutch oven brown them two by two over a high burner. (This may take slightly more oil.)
4. Remove the hens and reserve. Add the sausage and brown it well. Remove the sausage with a slotted spoon and reserve it.
5. Add remaining 2 tablespoons oil to the Dutch oven, lower the heat, and add the flour. Whisk it into a roux. Keep whisking for 7 minutes. The roux will turn a dark brown.
6. Add the vermouth and boil off the alcohol for a few seconds.
7. Add the tomatoes.
8. Place the hens flat on the bottom. They should fit snugly in a large Dutch oven.
9. Add the water and reserved okra-vegetable mixture.
10. Bring all ingredients to a boil, and simmer the gumbo for 45 minutes. Taste the stock for salt. (The sausage has seasonings so don't add salt before tasting.)
11. Add the oysters and their liqueur to the gumbo, and simmer only 4–5 minutes.
12. Serve the gumbo in large flat soup plates. First, dish out the hen halves and 2 oysters for each person. Then make sure each bowl has okra and sausage.

Serves 4

Hominy Buttermilk Soup

Hominy is dried corn that has been hulled after soaking in lye. It's meaty and mellow tasting. Use prepared canned hominy. Preparing it at home takes 5–6 hours.

1 T corn oil
¼ lb salt pork, cut into ½-inch
    pieces
½ C onion, peeled and minced
½ C pine nuts
2 C chicken stock

5 oz dried beef
Warm water
½ t cumin
2 C hominy (white or yellow),
    canned, drained, and rinsed
2 C buttermilk

1. In a large soup pot, heat the oil. Add the salt pork, and render the fat over medium heat. The pork will turn brown. Remove the pieces with a slotted spoon and discard them.
2. Add the onion to the fat and stir 1 minute. Reduce the heat. Cover the pot, and let the onion sweat for 5–8 minutes.
3. Place the pine nuts with the chicken stock in a blender, and thoroughly blend them to a creamy consistency.
4. Slice the dried beef into ½-inch strips, and soak them in a bowl of warm water.
5. With clean hands, squeeze the water from the dried beef strips, and add them with the cumin to the pot with the onion. Stir and sauté the beef over medium heat until it frizzles and curls.
6. Add the pine nut mixture to the beef and bring it to a boil. Reduce the heat and simmer for 5 minutes.
7. Add the hominy and buttermilk. Heat well but do not boil.

Serves 4

POULTRY

29

Jerusalem Artichoke Soup

Although cooked Jerusalem artichokes smell and taste like the hearts of the more familiar green, globe artichokes, they're a tuber of the sunflower family. The plants are easily grown in home gardens; we've dug up homegrown tubers for this soup. The name Jerusalem is an Americanization of the Italian girasole *(sunflower), which literally means to turn with the sun.*

¾ lb Jerusalem artichokes,
   peeled and cut into pieces
4 C chicken stock
3 T sweet butter
1½ T flour
½ t salt

Sprinkle of white pepper
1 t sugar
2 t dry sherry
1 egg yolk
2 T heavy cream

1. Boil the artichokes in the stock until they're tender (about 10 minutes).
2. In a separate large bowl, pass the artichokes and stock through a fine disc of a food mill to purée them.
3. In a medium-size saucepan over medium heat, melt the butter. Whisk in the flour and blend it into a smooth roux. Whisk the artichoke purée into the flour and simmer for 10 minutes. The stock must be stirred occasionally as it thickens.
4. Add salt and white pepper to taste. Add the sugar and sherry.
5. In a separate bowl combine the yolk and cream.
6. Remove 1 cup of the soup and, stirring constantly, slowly pour it into the yolk-cream mixture in the bowl. Return this to the rest of the soup. Simmer 5 minutes more.

Serves 4

KIELBASA CABBAGE SOUP

This soup has a deep, hearty flavor, which makes it a favorite choice on a cold, bone-chilling day.

3 C cabbage, cored and finely
   shredded
Salted water to cover
3 C chicken stock
3 C water
1 lb kielbasa Polish sausage, in
   ½-inch rounds
¾ C onion, peeled and diced

1 garlic clove, peeled, crushed,
   and minced
2 C whole tomatoes, peeled, with
   juice
½ t salt
2 t Hungarian paprika
½ C dry white wine

1. Cover the cabbage with water. Blanch the cabbage for 15 minutes over high heat in boiling saltwater.
2. Add all the other ingredients to another soup pot, and bring them to a boil. Reduce the heat to a simmer.
3. Drain the cabbage, and add it to the soup pot.
4. Cover the pot, and simmer the soup for 45 minutes at a low boil.

Serves 6

KISHIK

Kishik (or kishk or kishek) may not appeal to everyone, but it's worth a try in order to sample a cultural food staple prevalent in Syria and other Near Eastern countries. Kishik is produced by mixing ground bulgur wheat with yogurt, letting it dry in the sun, and sieving it into a fine powder.

¼ C olive oil
1 C onion, peeled and minced
1 garlic clove, peeled, crushed,
   and minced
⅔ C kishik

6 C chicken stock
Freshly ground black pepper
2 hard-boiled eggs
⅓ C parsley, de-stemmed and
   minced

1. In a large skillet, heat the olive oil over medium heat. Add the onion and garlic. Sauté them for a few minutes. Reduce the heat to low, cover, and let them sweat 5–8 minutes. Stir occasionally to prevent browning.

2.   Stir in the kishik and slowly add 5 cups of the chicken stock. Stir and
     bring the kishik to a boil. Reduce to a simmer and cook 7 minutes while
     stirring. The soup will become porridge thick. Add the remaining cup
     of chicken stock and the pepper to taste.
3.   Peel and chop the eggs. Mix the eggs with parsley, and serve them as a
     garnish on each portion.

Serves 6

&

LEEK SOUP

The leek is to the Welsh what laurel was to the Romans. Heroic Welsh sol-
diers wore it in their helmets and adopted it as their emblem. In the United
States this member of the onion family is sadly neglected. Served cold, this
soup is a vichyssoise.

**4 leeks (white part only), washed
    well and thinly sliced (approx-
    imately 1 fully packed C)
¼ C onion, peeled and diced
2 T sweet butter
2 C potatoes, peeled and diced**

**2 C chicken stock
1 ½ C half-and-half
⅛ t mace
1 t chervil
Salt
Sprinkle of white pepper**

1.   In a saucepan over medium heat, sauté the leeks and onion in the butter.
     Cover and let them sweat 5–8 minutes.
2.   Add the potatoes and the stock. Bring the stock to a boil.
3.   Cover the vegetables and simmer for 15 minutes.
4.   Work the vegetables and stock through a food mill using a medium-fine
     disc, or blend until fine but not puréed.
5.   Return the mixture to the rinsed pot and add the half-and-half.
6.   Season with mace, chervil, salt, and pepper to taste.
7.   Reheat the soup until hot.
8.   Serve piping hot, or refrigerate and serve chilled.

SOUPS
32

🙠

LEMONGRASS SCALLOP SOUP

Lemongrass is an exact description—blades of grass that taste like lemon. It may be found in most organic food stores. The essence of lemongrass produces a delicious, friendly stock for scallops. Be sure to cook the scallops only enough to turn them opaque or they'll turn tough.

2 T olive oil
2 T scallions (white part only), diced
1 garlic clove, minced
4 C chicken stock
¼ C parsley, de-stemmed and minced

½ C loosely packed dried lemongrass
3 drops hot chile sauce or Tabasco
¼ t soy sauce
¼ lb scallops, cut bite-size

1. In a large saucepan, heat the oil and lightly sauté the scallions and garlic for 2–3 minutes.
2. Add the chicken stock, parsley, lemongrass, chile sauce, and soy sauce. Bring the liquid to a boil, cover, and simmer the soup for 1 hour.
3. Strain the stock, discarding the vegetables.
4. Return the soup to the rinsed saucepan and bring it to a simmer. Add the scallops and cook briefly (about 1 minute).

Serves 4

🙠

LENTIL LEMON SOUP

Each bowlful of this soup is an entire meal of meat, potatoes, legumes, and green vegetables. The lemon juice and cumin are secret ingredients that elevate the lentil taste.

1½ C green lentils, washed
6 C water
2 C chicken or beef stock
1 lb Swiss chard (if unavailable, spinach), chiffonade
1 potato, cut into 1-inch pieces
⅓ C onion, peeled and diced
3 garlic cloves, peeled, crushed, and minced

4 T olive oil
2 T celery leaves, minced
¼ t coriander
Link pork sausage (2 per person)
Salt
Freshly ground black pepper
3 T lemon juice
½ t cumin

1. Bring the lentils, water, and stock to a boil in a large soup pot over high heat. (A soup bone may be added for extra flavor.)
2. Lower the heat to medium.
3. Wash and drain the chard. Remove the central stem, and slice layers of leaves into thin shreds (chiffonade).
4. Add the chard and potatoes to the stock. Slowly boil the soup, covered, for 45 minutes.
5. Add the onion and garlic to hot olive oil in a small skillet. Sauté them over medium-low heat for 3–4 minutes. Add the celery leaves and coriander.
6. Add this mixture to the soup.
7. Brown the sausages while the soup simmers another 5 minutes. (If the sausages are not precooked, start them with the onion.)
8. Stir in the salt, pepper, lemon juice, and cumin.
9. Serve in deep pottery bowls with 2 link sausages cut into each serving.

Serves 6

❧

LETTUCE SOUP

An elegant soup. The key is the right choice of lettuce—a buttery Boston type of lettuce cooks fast and enhances the creamy consistency.

**8 C Boston lettuce, finely shred-
  ded and tightly packed (chiffonade)
7 T sweet butter
4 T flour**

**2 C milk
½ t salt
3½ C chicken stock
½ t sugar
½ C heavy cream**

1. Four firm heads of Boston lettuce yield approximately 8 cups of chiffonade. Pick off the outer loose leaves; then wash each lettuce head by spreading the leaves and running water on them. Cut the heads of lettuce in half, core them, and roll the leaves tightly while cutting finely into shredded strips.
2. Make a béchamel sauce in a medium-size saucepan: melt 3 tablespoons of butter and whisk in the flour over low heat. Add the milk and salt, constantly whisking to prevent lumping and sticking. Simmer but don't boil the sauce until it is thick.
3. In a large bowl combine 2 cups of the béchamel, the chicken stock, and sugar.
4. Melt the 4 remaining tablespoons of butter in a casserole or soup pot. Add the lettuce, coat with butter, cover it, and cook it until the lettuce wilts (approximately 3 minutes).

5. Add the béchamel mixture to the lettuce and simmer it, uncovered, over medium heat for 10 minutes.
6. Place a food mill over a large bowl; with the fine disc in place, pass the soup through the mill.
7. Return the soup to the rinsed pot, add the cream, and heat the soup well; do not boil.

Serves 6

&

MADRILENE

This classic, delicately flavored soup is most suitable for a prelude to other fine dinner dishes. Be sure to press the soup through a strainer (a blender won't remove the tomato seeds). A handy substitute for a cheesecloth bouquet garni is to use a small stainless steel tea infuser or tea ball.

2 T sweet butter
⅔ C onion, peeled and diced
4 C. chicken stock
2 C. fresh tomatoes, peeled, cored, quartered, with juice
Bouquet garni (see right)
¼ C dry sherry
4 t arrowroot

2 T cold water
¾ t salt
Sprinkle of white pepper
4 t heavy cream

BOUQUET GARNI

⅛ t each rosemary, tarragon, marjoram
Strip of lemon peel

1. Melt the butter in a large saucepan over medium heat.
2. Add the onion, cover, and let it sweat for 5–8 minutes.
3. Add the stock, tomatoes, and bouquet garni. Bring to a low boil, cover, and simmer for 30 minutes.
4. Remove the bouquet garni. Strain the soup through a fine-mesh strainer. With a wooden spoon, press the tomato pulp mixture to extract all the juice.
5. Place the sherry in a small saucepan over high heat and reduce it to 2 tablespoons. Stir it into the soup.
6. In a small bowl, mix the arrowroot with the water.
7. Bring the soup to a boil, pour in the arrowroot mixture, and stir until thick. Add salt and pepper to taste.
8. Swirl a teaspoon of cream gently in each bowl to make a pattern on top of the soup.

Serves 4

MINTED PEA SOUP (CHILLED)

Most recipes for green pea soup, either hot or chilled, call for sugar, but you'll discover how naturally sweet fresh peas are without the addition. The mint should be fresh, not dried, for this totally refreshing soup.

2 C chicken stock
1 C water
¼ C mint (3 large sprigs)
3 C fresh peas, shelled
½ C onion, peeled and diced

½ C heavy cream
Salt
¼ C heavy cream, whipped
4 mint sprigs

1. Bring the chicken stock, water, and mint to a boil.
2. Drop the peas and onion into the rapidly boiling stock.
3. Reduce the heat, cover, and cook the peas at a low boil until tender (no longer than 12 minutes).
4. Cool and work through a food mill, using the finest disc. (A blender will not do in this case.)
5. Stir the cream into the purée.
6. Salt to taste.
7. Chill the soup in a pitcher.
8. If the soup separates, simply stir it well before pouring into chilled bowls.
9. Top with whipped cream and a small mint leaf sprig.

Serves 4

MISO

Miso is a paste made from fermented soybeans and sea salt, so the stock must be unsalted or the soup will be too salty. The Japanese use miso to enhance flavor and also as a thickener. The eye appeal in this simple soup is to see the finely cut vegetables at the bottom of the light, clear broth.

4 scallions
1 C fresh spinach leaves, well
    washed and de-stemmed
2 T safflower oil

4 C unsalted chicken or beef
    stock (or half of each)
1 T miso soybean paste
½ lb firm tofu, cut into small
    ½ -inch squares

1. Trim the scallions, leaving 3 inches of green leaves. Cut the scallions into small ¼-inch rounds.

2. Pack the spinach tightly to measure 1 cup; then shred (chiffonade).
3. Heat the oil in a soup pot over medium heat. Sauté the scallions for 2 minutes; then add the spinach and stir it until it wilts.
4. Add the chicken stock to the vegetables. Heat the soup.
5. Pour off ½ cup of the hot stock and mix in the miso paste.
6. Add the miso mixture to the soup. Heat it to boiling.
7. Divide the tofu into each bowl.

Serves 4

&○

MOLDED CHINESE SOUP

When we first heard of this concept, we couldn't understand why you would pour stock over an inverted bowl and exactly how this Chinese flower would stay together. Try it and you'll be amazed by the decorative charm of this creative soup.

1 large chicken breast, split
Water
1 dried Chinese mushroom
½ C warm water
6 oz cooked sandwich ham, sliced in ¼-inch wide strips
4 oz water chestnuts, rinsed, drained, and sliced
3 slices gingerroot, ¼ -inch thick

2 scallions, stems and all, cut into 1-inch pieces
Sesame or peanut oil
2 eggs, slightly beaten
8 – 10 whole snow peas, stems removed
4 ½ C chicken stock
Soy sauce

1. Steam the chicken breast over water in a steamer 7 – 10 minutes.
2. Tear the meat from the chicken and into shreds.
3. Soak the dried mushroom in warm water and remove the stem. Rinse and squeeze it like a sponge.
4. Prepare the ham, water chestnuts, gingerroot, and scallions. Refrigerate all the meats and vegetables until ready for use.
5. In an 8-inch skillet coated with oil, make 2 very thin omelettes one at a time. Slice them into long ½ -inch strips.
6. In a bowl with a bottom at least 6 – 8 inches in diameter, center the mushroom smooth side down. Arrange the chicken, ham, and egg strips alternately spiraling from the sides of the mushrooms. (Ingredients may be layered up the sides of the bowl too.) Fill in with the snow peas and scallions. Place the water chestnut strips at the center of the wheel.
7. Press the ingredients down tightly with the palm of your hand or a spatula. Cover them with ½ cup stock and sprinkle them with soy sauce.

8. Place a trivet in a large pot or wok with a cover. Fill the pan bottom with approximately 2 inches of water, and place the bowl of vegetables and meats on the trivet in the pan. Cover. Steam the vegetables in the bowl for 20 minutes.
9. In a separate saucepan, heat the chicken stock to a low boil. Select a large serving bowl that will hold the steamed vegetable bowl, or use your wok to serve the soup.
10. Invert the steamed vegetable bowl in the bottom of the serving bowl (as you would to turn out an upside-down cake). But don't remove the bowl-mold. Instead, pour the stock around the base of the inverted bowl. The suction of the liquid around the mold will release any vegetables that might stick to the bottom of the mold.
11. Now pry up the molded vegetable bowl with 2 spoons and carefully lift it off. The Chinese vegetables and meats will float in a circular molded shape in the stock.
12. Serve immediately at the table from the large serving bowl or wok.

Serves 4

&

MULLIGATAWNY

Mulligatawny is a south Indian word that literally means "pepper water," so the spicier the soup the better. Since peppercorns lose their potency after a year in the cupboard, the spices should be as fresh as possible. Cream of coconut is a purée similar in texture to fudge sauce. Half a teaspoon in each bowl lends an exotic flavor to this soup.

¼ lb salt pork, cut in pieces
1¾–2 lb chicken, cut into small
   frying pieces as for fricassee
½ C sweet green bell pepper,
   cored, seeded, and diced
⅓ C carrots, scraped and diced
⅓ C onion, peeled and diced
1 T flour
1½ t curry

3 peppercorns
2 cloves
1 small bay leaf
8 C water
1 C tomato sauce
½ t cayenne
Salt
Cream of coconut (optional)

1. Fry the salt pork to render fat but remove the lardoons (pork pieces).
2. In a heavy skillet, fry the chicken in the pork fat over medium-high heat.
3. Add the vegetables and sauté them for 5 minutes with the chicken.
4. Transfer the contents to a large soup pot or Dutch oven.

5. Mix the flour and curry powder. Sprinkle it evenly over the chicken and vegetables.
6. With the back of a knife, crush the peppercorns. Add them to the chicken with the cloves and bay leaf.
7. Cook the ingredients over high heat for 2 minutes. Add the water and bring it to a boil.
8. Simmer the soup, covered, for 1 ½ hours.
9. At the beginning of the last half hour, add the tomato sauce.
10. Remove the chicken pieces, cloves, and bay leaf. Work the vegetables and stock through a strainer or fine disc of a food mill.
11. Return the purée to the rinsed pot. Add the cayenne. Salt to taste.
12. Bring the soup to a boil. Meanwhile, discard the chicken bones. Skin and shred the chicken meat into bite-size pieces.
13. Add the chicken meat to the mulligatawny. Serve very hot with an accompanying bowl of fluffy white rice.

Serves 6

&

MUSTARD SOUP

This recipe for mustard soup is a variation of a fourteenth-century receipt from Le Viandier *compiled by Guillaume Tirel for Charles V's kitchen staff. It has a delicate flavor and smooth rich texture and is a wonderful first course for baked ham or a standing rib roast. Choose your favorite prepared mustard. The flavor permeates the soup and never dominates.*

2 T sweet butter	Sprinkle of white pepper
2 T flour	½ t onion juice (or grated onion)
2 ½ C chicken stock	2 egg yolks
1 C light cream (or half-and-half)	3 T light cream (or half-and-half)
½ C milk	3 T prepared mustard
Salt	

1. In a saucepan over medium heat, melt the butter and make a roux with the flour.
2. Add the chicken stock, 1 cup cream, and milk.
3. Add the salt and white pepper to taste. Add the onion juice.
4. Simmer the soup over low heat 10 minutes until the milk is scalded. Do not boil.
5. In a separate bowl, beat the egg yolks and 3 tablespoons cream until smooth.

6 Slowly add approximately 1 cup of the hot soup mixture to the egg mixture, whisking constantly.
7. Pour this liaison back into the pan with the rest of the soup, whisking constantly.
8. Reheat. Stir all the time for a smooth consistency. Never boil.
9. Add the mustard last, stirring it in.
10. Serve the soup in small portions.

Serves 6

𝔞

PANE E POMODORO SOUP

Bread soup has been a staple the world over. This version of Pane e Pomodoro *(bread with tomato) tastes best at the height of the harvest season with vine-ripe tomatoes and freshly picked basil.*

3 C chicken stock
4 C water
¼ C olive oil
2 garlic cloves, peeled, crushed, and minced
1 t fresh basil leaves, minced

½ lb sliced Italian bread exposed to the air for a few days
2 C fresh tomatoes, peeled, cored, and chopped, with juice
½ t salt
Freshly ground black pepper

1. Bring the chicken stock and water to a boil in a large soup pot.
2. Heat the olive oil in a large skillet.
3. Sauté the garlic and basil in the oil over medium heat. When the garlic turns golden, add the bread slices.
4. Press down on each slice of bread with a spatula to flavor and brown it lightly on each side. Remove the bread from the skillet.
5. Add the tomatoes to the skillet and boil them over high heat for 3 minutes. Add them to the hot chicken stock, cover the pot, and simmer the stock and tomatoes over low heat for 30 minutes.
6. Season with salt and pepper.
7. Place the bread slices in flat soup plates, and pour the tomato soup over the bread.

Serves 4

SOUPS

PARSLEY SOUP (CHILLED)

As an ever-popular garnish, parsley stimulates the appetite but only as a second billing. Here it is center stage.

2 T sweet butter
3 leeks (white part only), thinly
   sliced
4 ½ C chicken stock
¾ C dry white wine
1 ½ C potatoes, peeled and diced

Salt
Sprinkle of white pepper
1 C Italian parsley (flat leaf), de-
   stemmed and minced
1 C heavy cream

1. Melt the butter in a heavy soup pot over low heat.
2. Add the leeks and ¼ cup chicken stock. Sweat the leeks in the stock over low heat, covered, approximately 5 – 8 minutes.
3. Add the wine, potatoes, remaining 4 ¼ cups chicken stock, salt, and white pepper to taste. (If the chicken stock is heavily salted, adding more salt will be unnecessary.)
4. Cover the pot and simmer the soup over medium heat for 30 minutes.
5. Add the parsley and simmer it 5 more minutes.
6. Transfer the soup to a blender and purée in batches for 2 minutes each. Pour the soup into a large pitcher.
7. Stir in the cream.
8. Refrigerate the soup at least 2 hours or until it is well chilled, then pour it into individual bowls.

Serves 4

POULTRY

41

Parsnip Carrot Soup

This soup tames the woody texture and aggressive taste of parsnips. With the carrots, they make a mellow blend.

1 C parsnips, scraped and diced	2 C milk
1 C carrots, scraped and diced	⅛ t nutmeg
2 C chicken stock	½ t salt
1 T lemon juice	Orange slices

1. In a large saucepan, combine the parsnips, carrots, chicken stock, and lemon juice. Bring the liquid to a boil, cover, and cook at a low boil for 45 minutes.
2. Place the parsnip-carrot mixture into a blender with 1 cup milk. Blend for 2 minutes.
3. Return the mixture to the rinsed saucepan. Add the remaining cup of milk, nutmeg, and salt.
4. Heat. Do not boil.
5. Ladle the soup into bowls and garnish with orange slices.

Serves 4

Peanut Butter Soup

The combination of flavors in this soup (which is a takeoff of an African groundnut soup) will keep people guessing. The color is just as appetizing — a cross between a sunset and a peach.

⅔ C smooth peanut butter (all-natural)	5 C chicken stock
½ C tomato paste	¼ C heavy cream
⅓ C ripe banana, peeled and mashed	⅛ t cayenne (or more to taste)
	Salt

1. Place the peanut butter, tomato paste, and banana in a blender with 2 cups of the stock and blend well.
2. Pour the remaining 3 cups of stock into a medium-size saucepan.
3. Heat the stock. Add the puréed ingredients and cream.
4. Stir well. Add the cayenne and salt to taste. Reheat just to the boiling point.

Serves 4

POMEGRANATE SOUP

Pomegranates were cultivated originally in ancient Persia. This soup conjures some of the tastes and visions of that exotic and mystical country.

1 lb chicken quarters (leg and
thigh)
5 C water
¼ C celery, threaded and diced
4 scallions (white part only),
thinly sliced

1 t salt
3 pomegranates
1 lb eggplant, peeled and diced
2 T sugar
2 T fresh lime juice

1. Place the chicken in a soup pot. Add the water, celery, scallions, and salt. Bring the water to a boil, reduce the heat, and cover the pot. Simmer the ingredients for 20 minutes.
2. Meanwhile, cut the pomegranates in half, and carefully push the seeds from the integument and outer skin. Reserve the seeds in a bowl.
3. Using the medium-size disc of a food mill, process the seeds. This will provide about 1 cup of pomegranate juice.
4. Remove the chicken from the soup pot. Let it cool, then pick the meat from the bones. Discard the skin and bones. One pound of chicken quarters yields approximately 2 cups of chicken meat.
5. Add the pomegranate juice, chicken meat, and eggplant to the soup pot. Reheat the soup to boiling, cover the pot, and simmer it over medium heat for 20 minutes.
6. Stir in the sugar and lime juice.

Serves 4

POULTRY

POSOLE

Posole *is dried corn. Out West it is sold "prepared" (hulled and presoaked in lye). Cook prepared posole according to directions or use canned hominy. This quintessential Mexican dish is a thick, well-balanced dish. With nachos, warm tortillas, fry bread, or sopaipillas, it makes a complete meal.*

1 large chicken breast
1 lb country-style pork ribs
1 pork hock (unsmoked)
1 beef marrow bone
8 C water
2 T onion, peeled and minced
2 t salt
2 C hominy (prepared yellow or
  white), drained
2 C tomatoes, peeled, with juice

2 garlic cloves, peeled, crushed,
  and minced
1 T green jalapeño chile sauce
1 T chile powder
¼ t oregano

GARNISHES

½ C onion, peeled and diced
½ sweet green bell pepper,
  cored, seeded, and diced
1 C shredded lettuce

1. Place the chicken, pork ribs and hock, beef bone, water, onion, and salt in a large soup pot or Dutch oven. Bring the liquid to a boil. Reduce the heat, cover, and simmer for 1 ½ hours.
2. Remove the marrow bone and take out the marrow. Cut bite-size pieces of meat from the other bones, and add these with the marrow to the soup. Discard the bones.
3. Add the hominy, tomatoes, garlic, chile sauce and powder, and oregano. Correct for salt.
4. Simmer the soup another 30 minutes.
5. Place the garnishes on the table in small bowls and let people help themselves.

Serves 4 – 6

SOUPS

44

RED BEAN AND SAUERKRAUT SOUP

Be sure to rinse the sauerkraut so that this substantial, easy-to-make soup isn't overly salty. The bacon will be salty, too, so taste first before adding salt. As the soup cooks it will automatically thicken until it is almost stew-like. Serve it with a dark pumpernickel or rye bread for a complete meal.

3 T olive oil
½ C onion, peeled and diced
2 C turkey or chicken stock
2 ½ C water
2 C prepared red kidney beans, washed and drained
1 C potatoes, peeled and cut bite-size
1 C apple, peeled and cut bite-size

¼ C parsley, de-stemmed and minced
1 C sauerkraut, rinsed, drained, and squeezed by hand
6 peppercorns
¼ t mustard seed
1 C Canadian bacon, diced
Salt

1. Heat the oil in a large soup pot. Add the onion, cover, reduce the heat, and sweat for 5–8 minutes.
2. Add the stock, water, beans, potatoes, apple, parsley, sauerkraut, peppercorns, mustard seed, and Canadian bacon. Cover, bring to a boil, and cook for 1 hour. Stir occasionally.
3. Taste for additional salt.

Serves 4–6

POULTRY

45

Red Sweet Pepper Soup (Chilled)

This soup is sure to gather a legion of loyalists. It has a rich, red color and a tantalizing taste. Be sure to buy sweet globe bell peppers, not hot chile peppers. Red sweet peppers are green bell peppers that have ripened on the plant.

6 T sweet butter
2 C leeks (white part only), sliced
3 C sweet red bell peppers
   (approximately 1 lb of whole
   peppers), cored, seeded, and
   diced

2½ C chicken stock
Salt
Sprinkle of white pepper
2 C buttermilk

1. Melt the butter in a large saucepan and add the leeks. (One bunch of 4 medium-size leeks equals approximately 2 cups.) Cover the leeks and sweat them over low heat for 5–8 minutes.
2. Add the sweet red peppers, cover, and continue to sweat the vegetables 20 minutes or until they're limp. Place a piece of waxed paper under the lid to create a better seal.
3. Add the chicken stock and simmer the soup, covered, for 30 minutes.
4. Add salt and pepper to taste.
5. Cool and blend the ingredients in batches in a blender.
6. Add the buttermilk only when the soup reaches room temperature.
7. Place the soup in a covered container, and refrigerate it for 4 hours or until it is well chilled.

Serves 4

Risi-Bisi Chicken Liver Soup

Risi bisi (rice and peas) is a popular Italian dish. This soup is a cinch to prepare and also nutritious. Remember this one when fresh peas come into season in the spring. Place a bowl of freshly grated cheese on the table.

1 C chicken livers
2 T sweet butter
¼ C long-grain whole rice
2-3 C water
½ C shelled peas (fresh or frozen
   young peas)

4 C chicken stock
Salt
Freshly ground black pepper
Freshly grated Parmesan or
   Romano cheese

1. Sauté the chicken livers in the butter in a skillet over medium heat for 2 minutes. Cover, lower the heat, and simmer 5 minutes. Remove the skillet from the burner.

2. Meanwhile, place the rice in a large pot with the water, boil, lower the heat to a simmer, cover, and cook it for 20 minutes.
3. After the chicken livers are cool, remove and slice them into small bite-size pieces. Return the liver to the skillet with the pan juices.
4. Add the peas to the rice and boil them 8 minutes or until tender. (Extra water may be added if necessary.)
5. Strain the rice and peas.
6. Heat the chicken stock in a large saucepan.
7. Add the chicken livers, pan juices, rice, and peas.
8. Taste for salt and add a dash of pepper.

Serves 4

ॐ

ROSE-COLORED CAULIFLOWER SOUP

As Mark Twain said, "Cauliflower is cabbage with a college education."
Cauliflower is the mildest of the cabbage family, and this soup graduates
the compact, white-headed flower with honors.

2 ¼ lb cauliflower, cored and
 broken into florets (don't cook
 the stems)
Saltwater
1 T olive oil
3 rashers bacon, diced
½ C onion, peeled and minced

3 C chicken stock
2 T tomato paste
½ C half-and-half
¼ t paprika
1 C cheddar cheese, grated and
 tightly packed
Salt

1. Cook the cauliflower in boiling saltwater for 15 minutes or until it's fairly tender. Drain the cauliflower and reserve it.
2. In a heavy skillet, heat the olive oil and sauté the diced bacon in the oil over medium heat until the bacon pieces are crisp. Remove them with a slotted spoon and reserve them for a garnish.
3. Add the onion to the bacon drippings. Sauté the onion over low heat for 2–3 minutes. Cover the skillet and let the onion sweat 5–8 minutes.
4. Remove the onion with a slotted spoon and reserve.
5. Place 1 cup of the chicken stock, the tomato paste, and all of the drained cauliflower in a blender and purée until it is smooth.
6. Place the purée in a large saucepan. Add the remaining chicken stock, half-and-half, and paprika to the pan. Heat the soup over medium heat but do not boil it.
7. While whisking, slowly add the grated cheese to the soup. Whisk until the cheese is thoroughly melted. Taste the soup to see if it requires additional salt.
8. Sprinkle each serving with crisp bacon bits.

Serves 6

POULTRY

47

RUTABAGA SOUP

The common turnip often is maligned and neglected, but it has a delicate flavor paired with cream and a rich stock, raising it above its lowly status.

3 C rutabaga (yellow turnip),
    peeled and chopped
Water to cover
3 C chicken (or turkey) stock

½ C heavy cream
½ t salt
Sprinkle of white pepper
Sprinkle of grated nutmeg

1. Simmer the rutabaga for 25 minutes with just enough water to cover.
2. Drain the rutabaga, and place half of it in a blender with half the chicken stock. Blend for 2 minutes and pour the purée into a soup pot. Repeat with the remaining rutabaga and stock.
3. Add the cream, salt, pepper, and nutmeg.
4. Prewarm individual soup bowls with hot water. Drain them. Ladle the soup into the bowls.

Serves 4

SATEH SOUP

This soup transforms the traditional Indonesian peanut-coconut sauce into a delicious dish. Veal and pork may be substituted. Don't add too much harrisa. It is explosively hot.

2 chicken breasts, split
3½ C water
½ t salt
Marinade (see right)
1 C unsweetened coconut flakes
1 C boiling water
1 T sweet butter
1 garlic clove, peeled, crushed,
    and minced
¼ C onion, peeled and minced
1 t trassie (shrimp paste)
2 t brown sugar
½ C peanut butter, smooth and
    natural
1 C coconut milk (from above
    flakes)

3 C chicken stock (from above)
Salt
⅛ t harrisa (Indian chile sauce)

MARINADE

2 garlic cloves, peeled, crushed,
    and minced
2 t curry
1 t coriander
2 t miso (soybean paste)
¼ C fresh lemon juice
2 scallions (white part only),
    thinly sliced
Freshly ground black pepper

1. With poultry shears or a sharp knife, remove the bone and skin from the chicken breasts. Cut the meat into 1-inch pieces. Set it aside for the marinade. Place the chicken skin and bones in a medium-size saucepan with a lid. Add 3½ cups of water. Bring the water to a boil over high heat. Reduce the heat, and simmer the stock for 20 minutes. Strain out the chicken bones and skin, reserving the stock in a bowl. Stir in the salt.

2. Mix all the marinade ingredients together in a bowl large enough to hold the chicken pieces. Stir in the chicken so that the pieces are well coated with the marinade. Cover the bowl with a plate and set it aside for 1 hour.

3. Place the coconut flakes in a teapot. Add the boiling water. Stir once and let the coconut steep for 20 minutes. Strain off 1 cup of coconut milk, which you will use later.

4. Remove the chicken from the marinade and place it on paper towels, dabbing off the marinade. Push the chicken onto wood or metal skewers — 1 skewer for each person.

5. Place the skewers on a grill or wire rack 4 inches from the preheated broiler. Broil the chicken 6 minutes on one side.

6. Meanwhile, melt the butter in a heavy skillet over low heat. Add the garlic and onion, cover the skillet, and let them sweat 5–8 minutes.

7. Add the shrimp paste and brown sugar to the onion. Stir and cook it another minute or so.

8. Turn the heat to medium. Add the peanut butter and whisk as it bubbles, slowly pouring in the coconut milk until you have used all the milk and the mixture is smooth. Remove the skillet from the burner.

9. Turn the chicken skewers over, and broil the chicken on the other side for 4 minutes.

10. Return the peanut sauce to low heat. Slowly whisk in the 3 cups of chicken stock. Taste for salt. Add the harrisa.

11. Reheat the soup to a boil, but do not overheat it because the peanut butter may separate. Serve 1 skewer to each person, and eat the chicken in the soup or separately. If the skewers are metal, the cook must wear a pot holder to fork the chicken off the skewers for each guest.

Serves 4

SCALLOP SHRED SOUP

Shredding each scallop takes time but results in a delightful Chinese-style soup. Be sure to include a few peas in each serving.

6 C light turkey or chicken stock
½ lb sea scallops, washed thoroughly
3 thin slices of fresh, peeled gingerroot
¼ C fresh peas, shelled
3 T dry sherry

¼ t salt
Sprinkle of white pepper
2 T cornstarch
¼ C cold water
2 scallions, thinly sliced, including 1 inch of the green stalks

1. In a large saucepan, bring the stock to a low boil. Add the scallops and gingerroot. Cook, uncovered, for 2–3 minutes, and with a slotted spoon skim the top. Cover and cook at a low boil for 1 hour.
2. With a slotted spoon, remove the gingerroot slices and scallops. Discard the gingerroot. Run cold water over the scallops to cool them. Let them dry.
3. With your fingers, shred the scallops into very thin strips.
4. Cook the peas in the stock for 5–8 minutes over medium heat.
5. Return the scallop shreds to the soup. Add the sherry, salt, and pepper.
6. In a small mixing bowl, dissolve the cornstarch in the cold water.
7. Bring the soup to the boiling point. Stir in the cornstarch and simmer the soup for 5 minutes or until it is thickened and clear.
8. Serve with a few scallions in each bowl.

Serves 6

Scallop Soup, St. Jacques

The term St. Jacques once applied to scallops served in the shell. In this country scallops rarely are sold in the shell. Indeed, some "scallops" really are skate and other fish cut to look like scallops. Today the term St. Jacques is applied to most dishes combining scallops and cheese.

½ C dry white wine
½ C water
2 T shallots, peeled and minced
1 C chicken stock
Bouquet garni (see right)
¾ lb sea scallops, cut in bite-size
  pieces
2 T sweet butter
1 T flour
1 C light cream

¼ C grated Parmesan cheese
¼ C grated Gruyère cheese
1 egg yolk
Salt
Sprinkle of cayenne

BOUQUET GARNI:

4 peppercorns
1 bay leaf
1 parsley sprig

1. Bring the wine, water, shallots, and chicken stock to a boil in a large saucepan over high heat.
2. Add the bouquet garni in cheesecloth or tea infuser to the boiling stock.
3. Lower the heat and add the scallops. Gently simmer them in the liquid for approximately 10 minutes.
4. Discard the bouquet garni. Strain the liquid into a bowl, reserving the scallops and shallots in another bowl.
5. Melt the butter in a small saucepan over low heat and stir in the flour, making a roux. Whisk in the light cream slowly, and then the cheeses.
6. As soon as this Mornay thickens, remove it from the heat and whisk in the scallop stock.
7. Place the egg yolk, scallops, shallots, and 2 cups of Mornay mixture in a blender. Purée them for 1 minute.
8. Return all the ingredients to a large soup pot and heat them. Do not boil this soup.
9. Season with salt and cayenne to taste.

Serves 4

POULTRY

SCUNGILLI SOUP

Scungilli is the Italian name for conch, the giant sea whelk. It resembles the chewy texture of abalone and as a "tough customer" needs some pounding and marinating. If you wish to omit steps 1 and 2, and the 2 extra hours of steaming in step 6, use canned scungilli found in most Italian markets.

1 ¼ lb fresh or frozen conch
½ C lime juice
½ C cold water
4 C chicken stock
2 C whole Italian plum tomatoes, peeled, with juice
2 T pesto (minced basil and parsley in olive oil)

¼ t imported oregano
¾ C dry white wine
½ C spaghettini (thin spaghetti), broken into 1-inch pieces
Water
Salt

1. Cut the white-gray meat from the shucked conch into large pieces. Discard the foot of the conch, the valve, and the black sac. A pound and a quarter will yield about 2 cups of meat. Pound the conch well with a meat hammer for 2–3 minutes or until the meat is flexible and pulpy. Mince the conch meat with a mezza luna or a sharp knife. The smaller the mince, the more tender the scungilli.
2. Let the minced conch marinate in lime juice and water in a covered casserole for 1 hour. Drain and rinse it.
3. Bring the chicken stock and tomatoes to a boil in a large soup pot over high heat.
4. Heat the pesto over low heat in a medium-size stainless steel skillet. Add the oregano, and gently simmer the herbs a few minutes.
5. Add the scungilli and white wine to the skillet. Turn up the heat slightly, and simmer the scungilli for 15 minutes.
6. Add the scungilli and wine to the soup pot. Cover the soup and simmer it for 1 hour. Keep the pot covered, setting the soup aside at room temperature for a few hours. It will continue to cook in its own steam.
7. Shortly before serving, boil the spaghettini in water according to package directions or until it is al dente (firm to the bite).
8. Drain the pasta and add it to the soup. Correct the soup for salt.

Serves 4

SENEGALESE SOUP

Curry is a condiment composed of 10 to 16 spices. The basis for curry powder is the golden turmeric pod. More curry may be added to this recipe. When chilled the natural gelatin in the chicken stock may gel in the refrigerator. If it does, beat in a bit of half-and-half until the soup returns to the desired consistency.

2 T sweet butter
1 ½ T flour
2 t curry
3 C chicken stock
2 egg yolks

½ C half-and-half
⅓ C plain yogurt
1 C cooked chicken meat, shredded
Salt

1. Melt the butter in a large saucepan over low heat, and stir in the flour and curry to make a roux.
2. Slowly whisk in the chicken stock, and bring it to a boil over medium-high heat. Remove the pan from the burner.
3. In a separate bowl, whip the yolks, half-and-half, and yogurt together.
4. Pour this mixture in a thin stream into the curry stock, stirring constantly.
5. Add the shredded chicken to the soup. Salt to taste.
6. Return the soup to the heat, and simmer (but do not boil) for 15 minutes or until it thickens.
7. Serve hot or chilled.

Serves 4–6

POULTRY

SHARK'S FIN SOUP

Shark's fin is found in Chinese markets and looks somewhat like a mass of dried rawhide. This delicacy goes by the name of "needles" and when boiled looks like slightly cooked egg. Save this soup for a celebration when you have the extra time and money to enjoy it.

1 (7 oz) shark's fin cake (sometimes called "needles")
Cold water
2 scallions
2 slices gingerroot, peeled
¼ lb uncooked loin pork (from 1 loin chop), thinly sliced
2 t dark soy sauce
1 t rice wine
1½ t Oriental sesame seed oil
1 slice gingerroot, peeled and crushed with the side of a cleaver or pricked with a fork
5 T rice wine
1 egg white, whipped until foamy
1 t cornstarch

¼ lb uncooked, boned, and skinned chicken breast (from split chicken breast), thinly sliced
6 C chicken stock
2 T cornstarch
1 t sugar
2 T rice wine vinegar
2 t Worcestershire sauce
1 t gingerroot, peeled and minced
2 T thinly sliced scallions (bottom 3 inches)
¼ t Chinese hot chile sauce (or Tabasco sauce)
¼ lb cooked sandwich ham (½-inch strips, thinly sliced)

1. Place the shark's fin cake (needles) in a large pot. Add cold water to cover it. Add one scallion and a piece of gingerroot. Bring the fin to a boil over high heat. Cover the pot. Reduce the heat and simmer the fin for 45 minutes. Drain and rinse the shark's fin. Return it to the pot and repeat all of the above process.

2. In a bowl, marinate the pork strips in 2 teaspoons of soy sauce, 1 teaspoon of rice wine, and ½ teaspoon Oriental sesame seed oil.

3. In another bowl, soak the gingerroot in 1 tablespoon of rice wine for 5 minutes.

4. Remove the gingerroot and stir the egg white, cornstarch, and chicken into the rice wine. Set this mixture aside.

5. Heat the chicken stock over medium heat.

6. In a cup, combine the remaining 4 tablespoons of rice wine with 2 tablespoons of cornstarch, the sugar, and the rice wine vinegar.

7. In a separate bowl, mix the Worcestershire sauce, 1 teaspoon of minced gingerroot, remaining 1 teaspoon Oriental sesame seed oil, 2 tablespoons of scallions, and hot chile sauce.

8. Remove the gingerroot and scallions from the well-drained and rinsed shark's fin. Add the fin to the heated chicken stock.
9. Add the pork mixture, chicken mixture, scallion-seasoning mixture, and ham to the soup pot.
10. When the soup is just bubbling, stir the cornstarch once in the cup and add it to the soup. Slowly boil the soup for 2–3 minutes until the broth thickens and clears.

Serves 6

৵৹

SIZZLING RICE SOUP

Children will adore this soup. (And if they don't adore shrimp, substitute chicken.) Day-old steamed rice works better than freshly made. The drier the grains of cooked rice the better. The grains will be separate, but they will attract each other in the hot oil. Stand away when you drop the rice into the oil because if it isn't as dry as it should be the oil may splatter. Make sure that the rice is refried so it is absolutely hot at the last minute. Otherwise, it may fizzle instead of sizzle.

1 C cooked leftover unprocessed long-grain white rice
4 C chicken stock
½ C small edible pea pods, ends trimmed
½ C small cooked shrimp, de-veined and shelled
¼ C water chestnuts, rinsed, drained, and sliced
⅔ C safflower oil
3 scallions (white part and 1 inch of green stalk), trimmed and sliced

1. Preheat the oven to 300° F. Spread the rice evenly in an ovenproof pie plate or shallow dish. Place the rice in the oven to dry out for 15 minutes.
2. Heat the stock over medium-high heat. Add the pea pods, shrimp, and water chestnuts to the stock.
3. Meanwhile, in a wok heat the oil for frying.
4. Remove the rice from the oven and drop a grain into the hot oil. If it spins and puffs up, the oil is ready for frying.
5. Divide the rice into four portions. Take the first portion onto a spatula and place it in the oil.
6. The rice grains will coalesce into a sort of crust. Let the rice crust brown in the oil (about 1½ minutes). Turn over the crispy crust and fry it golden brown (another 1½ minutes).

7. Repeat with the other 3 rice portions.
8. Keep the oil hot and briefly refry all of the rice portions so that they're hot.
9. At this point the stock *must* be boiling.
10. For the desired effect, place the just-fried rice crusts in a large serving bowl. Immediately place the bowl on the table, and pour the boiling hot stock over the rice. It will sizzle.
11. Ladle one rice crust into each individual bowl, along with the pea pods, shrimp, and chestnuts. Place a small dish of scallions on the table for a garnish.

Serves 4

ৡৢ
SORREL SOUP

Sorrel looks like a spinach leaf and tastes like lemon. This soup is known as Potage Germiny *by the French. It is the pièce de resistance for a light special luncheon.*

¾ **lb sorrel**	**3 C chicken stock**
½ **C onion, peeled and diced**	**Salt**
¼ **C sweet butter**	**Sprinkle of white pepper**
1 egg yolk (extra large egg),	**Freshly grated nutmeg**
slightly beaten	
1 C light cream (or half-and-	
half)	

1. De-stem, rinse, and drain the sorrel leaves.
2. Stack the sorrel leaves. Then slice strips off the layered leaves (chiffonade).
3. In a saucepan over medium heat, sauté the onion in the butter. Add the sorrel and simmer, covered, until wilted, approximately 5–8 minutes.
4. In a separate bowl, beat together the egg yolk with the cream.
5. Boil the stock in a soup pot. Remove the stock from the heat, and slowly add the yolk mixture while stirring with a wire whisk.
6. Return the pot to low heat. Do not boil the soup.
7. Add the sorrel-onion mixture. Season the soup with salt and pepper.
8. Grate nutmeg on top of each serving.

Serves 4

SPINACH CELERY SOUP

Spinach Celery Soup *arouses the appetite. It is tasty and very high in iron. Popeye would like this one.*

½ lb fresh spinach
1 C celery, threaded and diced
2 T shallots, peeled and minced
1 C chicken stock
½ C spinach liquid
2 T sweet butter

1 T flour
2½ C milk
½ t tarragon
¼ t salt
Sprinkle of white pepper
2 T grated Parmesan cheese

1. Wash the spinach thoroughly and de-stem the leaves. Drain them well in a collander.
2. In a saucepan, bring the celery, shallots, and chicken stock to a boil. Cover and simmer them for 10 minutes.
3. Meanwhile, boil down the spinach in another pan. Do not add water. Cover and let the spinach wilt over medium to low heat for 5 – 8 minutes. Half a pound of spinach reduces to about 1 cup of wilted spinach.
4. Drain and press the spinach in a strainer, reserving the spinach liquid in a bowl.
5. Chop the spinach with a mezza luna or knife.
6. Over medium heat, melt the butter in a large saucepan. Add the flour to make a roux, stirring with a whisk. Slowly add the milk to the flour, and stir the béchamel (white sauce) for 5 minutes.
7. Add the celery-stock mixture, spinach, spinach liquid, and tarragon to the béchamel.
8. Stir in the salt and pepper.
9. Heat the soup to near boiling and whisk in the Parmesan cheese.

Serves 4

POULTRY

STRACCIATELLE

This quick and easy soup has a ragged look to it, the reason Italians call it
Stracciatelle — *"rags." The Chinese refer to it as egg-drop soup.*

2 eggs (room temperature)
1 T lemon juice
2 T grated Parmesan cheese
1 garlic clove, peeled and
   crushed

2 C chicken stock
2 C beef stock
¼ t salt
Freshly ground black pepper

1. Combine the eggs, lemon juice, cheese, and garlic in a bowl. Mix minimally with a fork so that the white and yolk of the eggs are still fairly separate.
2. Combine and simmer the stocks. Bubbles should not break the surface. You can also boil the stock and then turn off the heat.
3. Hold the egg mixture approximately 5 inches above the stock. Have a fork ready in the other hand. Pour the egg mixture in a slow, steady stream, and break it in midair with the fork. This will produce strands of egg in the broth.
4. Add salt and pepper to taste.
5. Serve the stracciatelle immediately.

Serves 4

SUGAR PUMPKIN CURRY SOUP

*Cooking pumpkins are smaller than the Halloween variety and are called
sugar pumpkins. You may carve a tureen out of a second small pumpkin,
scooping out the seeds and steeping it in boiling water for 5 minutes before
draining it and adding the soup.*

2 C fresh sugar pumpkin (a 2 ½
   lb pumpkin)
2 T sweet butter
3 T onion, peeled and minced
3 C chicken stock
1 C sharp Cheddar cheese,
   grated

⅔ C light cream
Sprinkle of white pepper
⅛ t freshly grated nutmeg
½ t curry
½ t salt

1. Cut the pumpkin in half and scoop out the seeds. Place the pumpkin halves face down on a piece of foil on a baking sheet, and bake 30–40 minutes at 350° F.
2. Scoop out and reserve the cooked pumpkin pulp. (If any is left over, it can be frozen.)
3. In a large saucepan over medium heat, melt the butter. Sauté the onion a few minutes, cover, and sweat 5–8 minutes.
4. Place 1 cup of pumpkin, 1 cup of chicken stock, and the cooked onion in a blender and purée for 1 minute.
5. Repeat with the remaining pumpkin and stock. Pour the purée into the rinsed saucepan.
6. Add the cheese and cream to the pumpkin purée. Heat the soup over a medium burner, stirring until the cheese melts.
7. Add the seasonings and taste for salt.

Serves 4

ॐ
SZECHUAN SOUP

This soup requires little cooking time if the stock is already prepared. About 20 minutes are spent preparing the meats and vegetables, stir-frying, and boiling. We prefer raw pork chops and snow peas, but a variety of ingredients may be substituted, including the chicken used to make the stock. Golden needles, wood ears, dark soy sauce, bean curd, and Chinese hot sauce may all be purchased at Chinese shops and in specialty sections of supermarkets. A word of caution—if the chicken stock is salted, not as much soy sauce is needed.

⅓ C pork, fish, or chicken (shredded if cooked, or sliced if raw)
1 T dry sherry
3 T cornstarch
2 T wood ears
2 T golden needles (dried daylily buds)
Boiling water
½ C water
2 T scallions, diced

1 C vegetable of choice (pea pods, celery, bok choy, cabbage, spinach)
2 T peanut oil
3½ C chicken stock
Soy sauce
2 T rice vinegar
¼ t Chinese hot sauce or Tabasco
½ C firm tofu (bean curd), cubed

1. Raw pork, fish, or chicken may be used, or leftovers. Slice the raw ingredients in fine 1-inch strips or shred cooked ingredients. Marinate the meat, fish, or fowl in sherry mixed with 1 tablespoon cornstarch while preparing the vegetables.
2. Soak the wood ears and golden needles in boiling water for 15 minutes. Snap off any hard pieces from the wood ears and hard stems from the needles. With clean hands, squeeze the water from both. Cut the needles in half, and slice the wood ears into thin 1-inch pieces.
3. Mix remaining 2 tablespoons cornstarch with ½ cup water.
4. Dice the scallions, and slice the vegetables into thin diagonal 1-inch strips.
5. Coat the wok or heavy skillet with peanut oil and heat for frying. Add the pork, fish, or chicken to the oil with the scallions.
6. Stir-fry for 2 minutes. Add the vegetables and stir-fry another 2 minutes. If frozen vegetables are used, cook them under a steamer cover. Stir and add the cornstarch mixture.
7. Add the chicken stock and soy sauce to taste. Mix the vinegar and hot sauce in a large serving bowl which has been preheated with hot water.
8. Pour the soup into the vinegar mixture. Szechuan soup is ladled into bowls at the table. Diners may help themselves to the bean curd.

Serves 4

&

TOMATO COUSCOUS SOUP

Couscous is a coarse-grain semolina made from hard wheat. When it is soaked, it turns into fluffy, delicate particles double in size.

1 ½ C chicken stock
¼ C couscous
2 T olive oil
¼ C onion, peeled and diced

2 C tomatoes, peeled, seeded, and chopped
¼ t imported oregano
¾ t salt

1. In a saucepan over high heat, boil ½ cup of chicken stock.
2. Place the couscous in a small bowl and pour boiling stock over it. Cover tightly with a plate or foil, and let it set for 20 minutes (the couscous will absorb the stock).
3. Meanwhile, heat the oil in a heavy saucepan and sauté the onion 2–3 minutes.
4. Add remaining 1 cup stock, tomatoes, and oregano. Cover and simmer until the tomatoes are tender, 20–25 minutes.
5. Add the salt. Stir in the couscous and stock mixture and reheat the soup.

Serves 4–6

Tomato Soup

Basic. Easy. Good. Garden-fresh tomatoes and herbs in season are best. Try dill or sorrel as a substitute herb. Add a little dry wine if you have some on hand. Double or triple the recipe, and freeze it as a foundation for other soups and sauces.

6–8 fresh ripe tomatoes, quartered
2 ½ C chicken stock
½ t basil
½ t thyme
¼ t imported oregano

¼ t salt
Sprinkle of white pepper
¼ C tomato paste
½ C cream, yogurt, or sour cream

1. In a medium-size saucepan, simmer the tomatoes in the chicken stock with the herbs for 15 minutes.
2. Pass this mixture through a sieve or fine disc of a food mill, and pour the purée back into the rinsed pot.
3. Add the salt and pepper. Taste for preferred seasonings.
4. Stir in the tomato paste.
5. Add the cream. (Yogurt or sour cream adds a different flavor.)
6. Heat. Do not boil.
7. Serve in bowls that offset the bright red color of the soup.

Serves 4

Tomato Yam Soup

Yams are sweeter than sweet potatoes. This soup has a down-to-earth flavor and a brilliantly shocking color.

3 small leeks (white part only), well washed and thinly sliced
2 T sweet butter
2 ripe tomatoes, peeled and seeded
2 ½ C chicken stock

½ t salt
½ t fresh basil, de-stemmed and minced
1 C fresh yam pulp, cooked (baked or boiled)
Salt

1. In a soup pot over low heat, sauté the leeks in the butter, cover the pot, and sweat the leeks for 5–8 minutes.
2. To peel whole tomatoes, drop them in boiling water first. Slice the tomatoes and add them to the leeks.

POULTRY

3. Add 1 cup of chicken stock, salt, and basil. Cover and simmer the soup for 10 minutes.
4. Place the stock, tomatoes, and leeks in a blender, and purée them for 2–3 minutes.
5. Return this mixture to the soup pot.
6. Blend the cooked yams with the remaining 1 ½ cups of chicken stock.
7. Add the yam mixture to the saucepan, and bring the soup to a boil.
8. Adjust for salt.

Serves 4

ॐ
TORTELLINI ESCAROLE SOUP

These days natural ricotta and meat tortellini may be found in freezer or pasta sections of most supermarkets. For a meat version, fry Italian fennel sausage and cut it into the soup. To convert to a vegetarian dish, simply leave out the bacon, substitute vegetable stock, and use cheese tortellini.

1 C tortellini
2 rashers lean bacon, diced
1 T olive oil
1 garlic clove, peeled, crushed,
    and minced
½ C sweet red bell pepper, cored
    and diced
2 C escarole, washed well and
    de-stemmed

4 C chicken stock
2 C Italian plum tomatoes,
    peeled and chopped, with juice
1 ½ C drained cooked white kid-
    ney (cannellini) beans
    (a 15-oz can)
¾ t salt
½ C grated Parmesan cheese

1. In a large saucepan with a lid, cook the tortellini according to package directions.
2. In a separate Dutch oven or heavy soup pot over medium heat, sauté the bacon in the olive oil for 3–4 minutes. Add the garlic and sweet red pepper and sweat, covered, for 5–8 minutes.
3. Prepare the escarole by washing the leaves and stacking them. Then slice into a chiffonade.
4. Stir the escarole into the bacon-garlic-pepper mixture. Cover the vegetables, and simmer them over medium heat for 10 minutes or until the escarole is completely wilted.
5. Add the stock and tomatoes to the soup and simmer it for 30 minutes.
6. Drain the tortellini and add with the beans to the soup. Stir in the salt. Place a bowl of freshly grated Parmesan on the table.

Serves 4

TROUT SOUP SOLIANKA

This colorful Russian fish soup is a sure candidate for promoting glasnost.
Any oily fish (salmon, sturgeon, mackerel) may be substituted for the trout.

4 trout (cleaned and filleted, with heads intact)
4 C cold water
1 C chicken stock
½ C clam juice
Bouquet garni (see right)
2 T sweet butter
½ C carrots, scraped and diced
½ C onion, peeled and diced
½ C celery, threaded and diced
1 garlic clove, peeled and crushed
½ C whole tomatoes, peeled, with juice
½ t salt
Freshly ground black pepper
2 T vodka
1 T capers

⅓ C fresh lemon juice (1 medium-size lemon)
1 t parsley, de-stemmed and minced
2 t fresh dill, de-stemmed and minced (¼ t dried dill may be substituted)
12 black pitted olives, coarsely chopped
Sour cream

BOUQUET GARNI

½ bay leaf
3 parsley sprigs
1 onion slice
4 peppercorns, crushed
3 celery leaf sprigs
¼ t dried thyme (or 1 fresh sprig)

1. Cut off the trout heads and small fins, and place them in a medium-size soup pot with the cold water, chicken stock, and clam juice. Add the bouquet garni. Cover the pot, and simmer this fish stock 20 – 25 minutes over medium heat. The stock will boil down to about 3 ¼ – 3 ½ cups.
2. Drain the stock through a fine strainer into a bowl, discarding the bouquet garni and fish trimmings. Reserve the fish stock.
3. In a large saucepan over low heat, melt the butter and sauté the carrots, onion, celery, and garlic for 5 minutes.
4. Cover the vegetables and simmer them for 10 minutes. Remove the garlic and discard.
5. Heat the fish stock in a soup pot. Add the sautéed vegetables and the tomatoes.
6. Season the soup with salt, pepper, vodka, and lemon juice. Bring it to a boil. Cover the pot and simmer the soup over medium heat for 10 minutes.
7. Cut each trout into three, then cut these pieces in half. Drop the trout into the soup and boil it gently for 2 – 3 minutes.
8. Take the solianka off the heat and add capers, parsley, dill, and olives.
9. Garnish each portion with a spoonful of sour cream, and serve another bowl of sour cream at the table.

Serves 6

POULTRY

TRUFFLE SOUP WITH PUFF PASTRY

Granted, this is an elaborate soup. It may take some practice, especially if you're not used to making puff pastry. Be sure to weigh the flour and to keep the butter between the flour layers chilled. The pastry must be tied down with kitchen string so it won't slip into the soup.

½ split chicken breast
Water to cover chicken
Mirepoix (see right)
2 T olive oil
Pinch of thyme
1 ¼ C chicken stock
1 T dry white vermouth
1 C light beef stock
Salt
Freshly ground black pepper

Puff pastry for 4 (see following recipe)
1 egg, well beaten

MIREPOIX:

2 T celery, threaded and minced
2 T carrots, scraped and minced
4 T mushrooms, de-stemmed, peeled, and minced
3.7-oz can of truffles, minced (reserve juice)

1. Place ½ of a split chicken breast in a large saucepan with water to cover it (approximately 2 cups). Over medium-low heat, let the chicken poach for 12 – 15 minutes. Remove the chicken breast and reserve the stock. Discard the skin and bones. Dice the meat and reserve it.
2. Prepare the mirepoix. Place the minced vegetables in a bowl with the reserved truffle juice.
3. Heat the olive oil in a small skillet over medium-low heat, and sauté the mirepoix and thyme 2 – 3 minutes.
4. Add ¼ cup of chicken stock and the vermouth. Cover the skillet, and let the mirepoix simmer for 10 – 12 minutes.
5. Combine remaining 1 cup of chicken stock and the beef stock. Taste the stock for salt and add it if necessary. Pass the pepper mill over the saucepan a few times. Heat the stock.
6. Divide the mirepoix and chicken meat evenly between 4 ovenproof dishes (ramekins) that are approximately 4 inches wide and 2 inches high with straight sides. (Individual soufflé dishes work well.) Add ½ cup of hot stock to each dish.
7. See the following recipe for the puff pastry. Roll the pastry ¼-inch thick. Cut out 4 circles ½-inch larger than the top of each dish. Brush the rounds with beaten egg. Invert the rounds on top of the dishes, and secure them tightly with kitchen string.
8. Place the soup dishes on a baking sheet. Bake the soup with pastry in a preheated 500° F. oven for 5 minutes. Reduce the heat to 350° F. and bake it another 5 minutes. Check periodically to see that the pastry isn't getting too brown.
9. Cut the strings and remove them from the dishes. Serve the soup at once.

Serves 4

½ lb sweet butter, room temperature
½ lb unbleached all-purpose
flour

½ t salt
½ C cold water
1 egg, slightly beaten

1. With your hands, shape the butter into a single rectangle about 4 x 6
   inches. Chill it.
2. Weigh the flour. Place it in a bowl and mix in the salt. Gradually stir in
   the water until the dough forms a ball.
3. On a flat surface, knead the dough 3–4 minutes until it is smooth and
   slightly elastic. (It should not be sticky.)
4. Roll the dough into a large rectangle about 6 x 16 inches and about ¼
   inch thick.
5. Place the chilled butter in the center third of the dough, shaping the butter to fit at least ½ inch short of the edges of the dough.
6. Fold the top third of the dough over the butter. Fold the bottom third of
   the dough over these layers. Seal the edges by pressing firmly with your
   fingers. Cover and refrigerate the dough for at least 15 minutes.
7. Follow this roll-and-fold step *four times*: place the dough on a floured
   surface with the seam side of the dough to your right. Roll gently but
   steadily to the original size rectangle of 6 x 16 inches. Work quickly,
   being careful not to break the butter through the dough. If the butter
   breaks through the top or bottom, pat flour onto the butter and finish the
   step. Don't flatten the dough too hard or too fast. Fold the top third over
   the center. Fold the bottom third over these two layers. Cover and chill.
8. Now the pastry is ready to form. To use for this soup, roll the dough
   into a squarish shape large enough for 4 rounds at least 4 ½ inches in
   diameter. Place the top of the bowl on the pastry, and cut the dough
   around it so that enough pastry will hang over the side of the dish to tie
   it with string.
9. Brush the pastry rounds with the egg. Pour the soup in the dish (*see*
   soup instructions). Turn the pastry over and center it over the top of the
   dish; the egg-brushed side is now underneath.
10. Press the edge of the pastry around the dish, sealing in the soup. With
    string, anchor the pastry around the rim of the dish, and tie it.
11. See step 8 on page 64 for baking instructions.
12. Option: for a glaze, you may brush on a mixture of 1 egg beaten with 1
    tablespoon of water immediately before you place the pastry in the
    oven.

TURKEY SOUP PAPRIKESH

Hungarian paprika adds a vibrant spiciness that will whet your palate for another serving of this sturdy soup.

2 T olive oil
1 fresh turkey leg and thigh, separated
¼ C onion, peeled and sliced
3 C chicken stock
3 C water
2 C celery, threaded and diced
2 C carrots, scraped and diced
2 garlic cloves, peeled, crushed, and minced

2 C potatoes, peeled and diced
½ C sweet green bell pepper, cored, seeded, and diced
1 C whole tomatoes, peeled, with juice
2 T Hungarian paprika
1 ½ t salt
Freshly ground black pepper
2 T flour blended with 2 T water

1. Heat the oil in a large soup pot over high heat. Brown the turkey pieces on all sides. Remove the turkey and reduce the heat.
2. Add the onion and sauté 2–3 minutes.
3. Add the stock, water, celery, carrots, garlic, potatoes, green pepper, and tomatoes. Bring the liquid to a boil.
4. Stir in the paprika, salt, and pepper. Add the browned turkey last. Bring the soup to a boil, then reduce the heat and simmer, covered, for 45 minutes.
5. Remove the turkey. Cut the meat from the bones, and return the meat to the soup. Discard the skin and bones.
6. Bring the soup to a boil, and add the flour-water mixture to thicken. Simmer 5 more minutes.

Serves 4

SOUPS

꙳

VEAL MOUSSE SOUP

The timbalelike mousse adds an extra special touch to this delicious soup. If you wish, substitute deboned chicken breast for the veal.

½ lb uncooked veal, sliced scal-
lopini style
3 eggs
½ C grated Parmesan cheese
⅛ t salt
Freshly ground black pepper
1 T olive oil

1 garlic clove, peeled, crushed,
·and minced
½ lb fresh spinach, well washed
and de-stemmed
4 C chicken stock (or half-
chicken and half-veal stock)

1. Place the veal in a food processor (or a blender) with the eggs, adding them one at a time. Purée them into a paste. This will take approximately 30 seconds.
2. Add the grated Parmesan to the veal and blend another 30 seconds. Add the salt and sprinkle of pepper. Purée another few seconds.
3. Heat the olive oil in a large soup pot over medium heat.
4. Add the garlic to the oil. Sauté it for a few seconds, then add the spinach. Cover the pot.
5. Cook the spinach over medium-low heat, stirring it occasionally. It should be wilted in 5–8 minutes.
6. Drain the spinach in a strainer, pressing out the juice with a spoon.
7. Place the spinach on a chopping board, and chop it well with a mezza luna or sharp knife.
8. Butter 4 custard cups (or ovenproof individual molds). Place 1 tablespoon of spinach in the bottom of each cup.
9. Add the veal mixture, leaving some space at the top of the cup. Place the cups in an ovenproof container with shallow sides. Fill the container with water so that it reaches halfway up the sides of the cups.
10. Place the cups in a preheated 325° F. oven for 15 minutes. Test the mousse with a knife. The knife should come out clean; when it does, the mousse is ready.
11. Heat the stock to boiling. Ladle the stock into each bowl. Loosen the mousse from the cups by running a knife along the edge. Invert the cup or mold over the soup bowl so the mousse falls into the stock, spinach side up.

Serves 4

WATERCRESS SOUP (CHILLED)

Watercress grows wild in brooks and freshets in many states, and thank goodness there is no such thing as canned, frozen, or freeze-dried cress. It has to be fresh to give that perky, sensationally uplifting taste. Use any left-over cress for bread-butter-watercress canapés.

2 ½ C watercress leaves   ⅓ C sour cream
3 C chicken stock   Salt

1. Wash and drain the watercress leaves (no stems).
2. Make sure to skim the fat from the chicken stock. Place 2 cups of stock in a blender with the cress and purée well.
3. Add the cress liquid to the remaining 1 cup of stock.
4. Whisk in the sour cream and add salt to taste.
5. Chill thoroughly and serve in glass bowls or water goblets.

Serves 4

WHITE ONION WINE SOUP

We have made this soup with a combination of Gruyère mixed with a strong Tilsit when Cantal cheese was unavailable. However, after the cheese is melted, the soup must be served at once before the cheese reverts to its basic texture.

2 C white onion, peeled and   1 ½ C dry light white wine (such
   diced   as Folle Blanche)
3 T sweet butter   ½ lb grated Cantal cheese
3 C chicken stock   Salt
                        Sprinkle of white pepper

1. In a large saucepan over medium-low heat, sauté the onion in butter. Cover and simmer over low heat approximately 10 minutes, stirring occasionally.
2. Whirl the onion in a blender just 1 second with 1 cup of chicken stock.
3. Return the onion to the soup pot with the remaining chicken stock.
4. Boil gently for 10 minutes, covered.
5. Add the wine. Boil gently for 5 minutes, uncovered. (The alcohol content of the wine should not be apparent. If it is, heat until it is evaporated.)
6. Over low heat, stir in the grated cheese until it is completely melted.
7. Add the salt and white pepper to taste. (Cheese has salt, so taste the soup first.)
8. This soup may be served with croutons.

Serves 4

Winter Melon Soup

Dark green winter melons are stocked in Chinese markets from November through February. They grow as large as watermelons and are lightly covered with a fine white powder. The transparency of the melon makes this a magical appetizer that transcends the ordinary.

2 chicken quarters (leg plus
  thigh)
6 C water
1 t salt
4 dried black mushrooms
1 C warm water
4 C winter melon (approximately
  a 3-lb slice of melon), peeled
  and cubed

1 garlic clove, peeled, crushed,
  and minced
1 t sugar
1 T light soy sauce
2 t peanut oil
2 scallions (white part and 2
  inches of green part), cut into
  ½-inch rounds
1 slice gingerroot, peeled and
  minced

1. Place the chicken quarters in a soup pot with the water, and bring it to a boil. Cover, reduce the heat, and simmer for 25 minutes. Add the salt.
2. Soak the dried mushrooms in warm water. Weight them down with a small saucer so that they're completely immersed. Soak them for 15 minutes.
3. While soaking the mushrooms, prepare the melon.
4. Drain the mushrooms and squeeze out the excess water by hand. Slice each mushroom into slivers from the stem. The stems are tough, so be sure to discard them.
5. Remove the chicken from the stock and let it cool.
6. Mix the garlic, sugar, and soy sauce in a bowl.
7. Remove the skin from the chicken, and shred off bite-size pieces of the meat. Place 1 cup of the chicken meat in the bowl with the soy sauce marinade. Set it aside for 15 minutes.
8. Add the winter melon and mushrooms to the stock. Return the stock to a boil; then lower the heat, cover, and cook the soup at a low boil for 30 minutes or until the melon turns translucent.
9. Heat the peanut oil in a wok or a small skillet. Sauté the scallions and gingerroot in the hot oil for 1–2 minutes. Pour off the excess oil. Add the chicken-soy sauce mixture, and swish it around to clean the skillet; then add the entire mixture to the stock.
10. Serve in Chinese rice bowls or lacquered bowls.

Serves 6

WONTON SOUP

These little packets of filling are easier to make than it may seem, once you get the pattern. Packages of wonton wrappers are available at most large markets, and folding instructions are usually on the package.

2 center-cut pork chops
   (about 1 lb)
1 T oil
1 ½ T scallions (about 4 scal-
   lions), finely sliced
2 T Chinese cabbage, finely
   shredded
¼ t gingerroot, peeled and
   grated

¼ t soy sauce
10 drops dark sesame oil
2 eggs (slightly beaten, each in
   separate bowls)
Wonton wrappers
10 C water
4 C chicken stock
¼ t salt

1. Remove the pork meat from the bone. Trim off the fat. Cut the pork into small pieces, and grind them through a meat grinder.
2. Heat the oil in a skillet over medium heat and sauté the ground pork 10 minutes or until it turns white and no pink tinge remains. Remove the pork with a slotted spoon to a large bowl.
3. Add 1 tablespoon scallions, the cabbage, gingerroot, soy sauce, sesame oil, and 1 slightly beaten egg to the pork and mix them well.
4. Prepare the wontons by filling and folding each wrapper this way: with your fingers, dab a little of the second beaten egg on 2 edges of each wonton wrapper. Place a generous teaspoon of filling off center and fold the wrapper over, pressing tightly at the egg-dabbed edges to seal it. Overlap the other 2 ends, and press into the center of the wonton.
5. Boil the water in a large pot. Place a third of the wontons at a time in the water, and boil each batch 5 minutes. Remove them with a slotted spoon and reserve.
6. In a wok or large soup pot over high heat, boil the chicken stock and add the salt.
7. Add the wontons to the stock and heat them thoroughly. Ladle 4 wontons with some stock into each bowl. Sprinkle the remaining ½ tablespoon of chopped scallions on the servings.

Serves 4

SOUPS

70

FISH

Basic Fish Stock (Fumet)   72

&

BASIC FISH STOCK (FUMET)

Fish stock is strong and may be diluted with water or other liquids. Local fish markets usually freeze fish heads and parts and give them to customers for making fish stock.

2 lbs fish heads (gills removed), tails, scraps
2 small celery stalks
4 parsley sprigs
¾ C dry vermouth

4 peppercorns
1 medium-size onion (or 6 shallots), peeled and chopped
7 – 8 C water (to cover the fish)

1. Combine all the ingredients in a large saucepan. Bring the liquid to a boil.
2. Reduce the heat and slowly boil, uncovered, 15 – 20 minutes.
3. Strain through a double layer of wet cheesecloth.

Yields approximately 7 – 8 cups

SOUPS
72

BAKED BLUEFISH CHOWDER

Bluefish is a dark, inexpensive, meaty-type fish. This one-pot meal dresses it up with mushrooms and cream into a palatable chowder.

Olive oil
¾ lb bluefish fillet, cut into 4
   pieces
4 T sweet butter
1 C mushrooms (3 large caps),
   de-stemmed, peeled, and
   chopped
¼ C onion, peeled and finely
   diced

2 potatoes, peeled and diced
2 C water
¼ C dry white vermouth
½ t salt
Freshly ground black pepper
1 T parsley, de-stemmed and
   minced
1 C light cream

1. Preheat the oven to 450° F. Lightly coat the bottom of a Dutch oven or ovenproof casserole with olive oil. Place the bluefish in the bottom, skin side up.
2. Meanwhile, in a large skillet over medium heat, melt the butter. Add the mushrooms, stir, cover, and sweat them for 3 minutes.
3. Add the onion, cover, and sweat the vegetables for 5 minutes.
4. Add the potatoes, water, and vermouth. Bring them to a boil, lower the heat, cover, and simmer for 8 minutes. Add the salt and pepper to the potatoes.
5. Lower the oven temperature to 375° F.
6. Pour the potato, onion, and mushroom broth over the fish in the Dutch oven, making sure the vegetables are covered by the liquid. Sprinkle on the parsley, cover, and bake the fish for 30 minutes.
7. Remove the Dutch oven and add the cream to the fish. Cover and return the fish for another 10 minutes.
8. Serve a piece of fish in each bowl with the vegetables and broth.

Serves 4

FISH

Baked Caribbean Fish Soup

This fish soup has a definite chile zing, although the long wax peppers are much milder than jalapeños. Try it for the first course of a fiesta-style dinner.

3 T olive oil
1 lb halibut steak
4 scallions (white part plus 1 inch of stalk), diced
2 tomatoes, cored, cut in eighths
½ C long yellow wax or Anaheim pepper, cored, seeded, and diced

¼ t ground chile pepper
¼ t salt
Freshly ground black pepper
¼ C fresh lime juice
2 C fish stock
1 C water
½ C dry white vermouth

1. Preheat the oven to 400° F.
2. Spread the olive oil on the bottom of a 10-inch Dutch oven. Place the halibut in the oil.
3. Sprinkle the scallions around the perimeter of the halibut. Place the tomatoes on top of the scallions in a circle on the outer edge.
4. Sprinkle the diced yellow wax pepper, chile pepper, salt, and black pepper over the halibut.
5. Pour the lime juice, stock, water, and vermouth over the halibut.
6. Cover the Dutch oven or casserole and place it in the preheated oven. Reduce the heat to 350° F. and bake for 30 minutes.
7. With pot holders, take the Dutch oven to the table to serve. Place a portion of the halibut in each bowl, and ladle the broth and vegetables over it.

Serves 4

CACCIUCO

When more squid is added to this Italian fish dish, it becomes a stew. Have the fishmonger cut the squid as if for fritto misto *(into the shape of onion rings). Serve with Parmesan cheese and hot, crusty Italian bread.*

2 T olive oil
¼ C parsley, de-stemmed and
    minced
½ C onion, peeled and diced
2 garlic cloves, peeled, crushed,
    and minced
⅛ t marjoram
⅛ t thyme

1 lb fresh squid, cut into ½-inch
    rings
1 C tomatoes, peeled, cored, and
    chopped, with juice
½ C tomato sauce
½ C dry white wine (or dry
    white vermouth)
1¾ C water
¼ t salt
Freshly ground black pepper

1. Place the olive oil in a soup pot over medium heat.
2. Add the parsley, onion, garlic, marjoram, and thyme. Sauté 1 minute.
3. Cover the pot and let the herbs and onion sweat 5 minutes.
4. Add the squid. Cover and simmer 7 minutes, stirring occasionally.
5. Add the tomatoes, tomato sauce, wine, and water.
6. Simmer, covered, 40 minutes over medium heat.
7. Add the salt and pepper to taste.

Serves 4

CIOPPINO

Cioppino (pronounced chop-eeno) is Italian for a spicy fish stew. You'll find this deeply satisfying and full of invigorating taste. The fish and shellfish should be absolutely fresh, glistening, and without any "fishy" aroma.

½ C olive oil
1½ C onion, peeled and diced
3 garlic cloves, peeled, crushed,
    and minced
½ C sweet green bell pepper,
    cored, de-seeded, and diced
1½ t imported oregano
4 fresh basil leaves, minced
2 C Italian plum tomatoes,
    peeled, with juice

2 T hot chile sauce
2 T tomato paste
1½ C Chianti
2 C bottled clam juice
1½ lb meaty-style fish (bluefish,
    monkfish, halibut, hake)
½ lb medium-size shrimp,
    shelled and de-veined
½ t salt
Freshly ground black pepper

1. Heat the oil in a large stainless steel or enamel soup pot.
2. Over medium heat, sauté the onion, garlic, sweet pepper, oregano, and basil in the oil for 2 – 3 minutes.
3. Lower the heat, cover, and let the vegetables sweat for 5 – 7 minutes, stirring occasionally.
4. Add the tomatoes, chile sauce, tomato paste, Chianti, and clam juice.
5. Bring the soup to a boil and simmer it for 10 minutes.
6. Cut the fish into bite-size pieces, and add it and the shrimp to the soup.
7. Simmer, uncovered, for 5 minutes. Do not boil.
8. Add the salt and pepper to taste.

Serves 4 – 6

🜲

CLAM AND TOMATO BROTH (CHILLED)

Piquant and seacoast tasty, this is easy to prepare at a vacation cottage before a main course of fish and chips.

2 C clam juice	1 T celery, threaded and diced
1 C fresh tomato juice	2 – 3 drops Tabasco sauce
½ t grated onion	2 t cornstarch
1 t fresh lemon juice	¼ C cold water

1. Place the clam juice, tomato juice, onion, lemon juice, celery, and Tabasco in a blender and blend well for 1 minute.
2. Pour the soup into a saucepan and heat to the simmering point.
3. In a measuring cup, dissolve the cornstarch in the water. Stir this mixture into the soup and bring it to a low boil. Cool.
4. Refrigerate the soup until well chilled.

Serves 4

CLAM CORN CHOWDER

New England clam chowder has many variations, including flour for thickening. Substitute diced potatoes for the corn in this recipe if you like, or adjust the measurements to include both. Bottled clam juice and frozen clams (sometimes with preservatives) are available. But, of course, fresh clams make the best chowder.

15 cherrystone clams	Reserved clam juice
2 C water	1½ C milk
1 T olive oil	½ C heavy cream
⅓ C salt pork, diced	¼ t salt
½ C onion, peeled and diced	Sprinkle of white pepper
1 C fresh corn, cut from the cob	2 T sweet butter

1. Scrub the clam shells with a wire brush. Place 1 cup water in a steamer, place the clams on a rack, cover, and steam the clams until the shells open slightly (about 4 – 7 minutes). Cool. Discard any clams that didn't open.

2. Over a bowl with a strainer on top, shuck the clams. Using a shucking knife or a strong paring knife, place the clam in your hand. Wear a glove or towel. Slip the blade into one end of the shell and pry it open. If the clam juice was lost in the steam water, strain it to use in the soup. Cut off the hard yellow clam muscle and discard it. Chop the rest of the clam, and reserve it for the chowder.

3. In a saucepan or soup pot, heat the oil. Add the salt pork and fry it over medium heat for 2 – 3 minutes. With a slotted spoon, remove and discard the pork dice, retaining the oil and rendered fat.

4. Add the onion to the oil. Cover, lower the heat, and sweat the onion for 5 – 8 minutes.

5. Add the corn and sauté 1 minute.

6. Combine water and the reserved clam juice so they equal 1 cup. Add it to the corn, and simmer another 4 minutes.

7. Add the milk and cream. Stir in the salt and pepper to taste. Reduce the heat, and bring the soup just below a boil.

8. Add the chopped clams and simmer them for 3 – 4 minutes. Ladle the chowder into individual serving bowls and top each with a teaspoon of butter. Serve with oyster or soda crackers.

Serves 4 – 6

CORN SCALLOP CHOWDER

This chowder is filling and notable for the mixed texture of crisp corn kernels and scallops. Try to find the pinkish, small, flavorful New England bay scallops. A word of caution. Some fish markets cut rounds from skate and other fish and pass them off as scallops. These imitation scallops tend to be uniformly round, unlike the real bay variety.

4 C water	1 C potatoes, peeled and diced
1 lb scallops	1 C fresh corn kernels
2 T sweet butter	1 bay leaf
1 C onion, peeled and diced	½ t salt
½ C celery, threaded and diced	Sprinkle of white pepper
1 T flour	2 C milk
	½ C sour cream

1. In a soup pot over high heat, bring the water to a boil. If using large sea scallops, cut them into bite-size pieces. Add the scallops to the water and simmer for 5 minutes.
2. Strain the liquid into a bowl and reserve. Set the scallops aside in another bowl.
3. Return the scallop liquid to high heat, and reduce it to 2 cups by boiling it.
4. Melt the butter in a heavy pot. Sauté the onion and celery in the butter 2 – 3 minutes. Whisk in the flour to make a roux.
5. While whisking, add the scallop liquid, potatoes, corn, bay leaf, salt, and white pepper.
6. Simmer, covered, for 10 – 15 minutes. Test the potatoes to see if they are cooked. Remove the bay leaf.
7. Over medium heat, warm the milk in a saucepan until tepid and whisk in the sour cream. (If the milk gets too hot, the sour cream will curdle.)
8. Add this milk mixture to the soup pot along with the scallops.
9. Taste the chowder for salt and pepper.

Serves 4

SOUPS

CRAB CHAMPAGNE SOUP

This rich, chowderlike appetizer is quick to fix and a good excuse to pop a champagne cork. Frozen crabmeat may be substituted. Three days old is the maximum for freshly picked crab; make sure to check the date on the carton.

½ C fish stock
½ C water
1 C brut champagne

1 C heavy cream
½ lb fresh crabmeat
1 ½ t chives, minced

1. In a large saucepan over high heat, bring the fish stock and water to a boil.
2. Meanwhile, in a separate small saucepan, bring the champagne to a low boil for a few seconds. Pour it into the stock mixture.
3. Remove this stock from the heat and stir in the cream.
4. Stir in the crabmeat and return it to low heat for 30 seconds, stirring constantly.
5. Add the chives.

Serves 4

FISH

79

CRAB GUMBO

This feisty New Orleans gumbo may be served over rice. The crabmeat acts as a thickener, and more may be added, depending on the desired consistency.

2 T oil
1 rasher lean bacon, diced
½ C sweet green bell pepper, cored and diced
½ C onion, peeled and diced
1 C okra, ends trimmed, sliced in ½-inch pieces

⅛ t thyme
1 C tomatoes, peeled and cored, with juice
1 C clam juice
3 C water
6–8 oz fresh crabmeat
2–3 drops of Tabasco sauce
½ t Worcestershire sauce

1. Place the oil with the bacon in a heavy soup pot over medium-high heat.
2. Add the pepper, onion, okra, thyme, and tomatoes. Sauté 1 minute, stirring constantly. Lower the heat.
3. Cover the vegetables and bacon, and let them sweat for 10 minutes, stirring occasionally.
4. Add the clam juice and water. Cover and simmer for 40 minutes.
5. Add the fresh crabmeat, Tabasco to taste, and Worcestershire sauce. Simmer 2 minutes more.

Serves 4

CRAB SOUP

Simple. Fast. No fuss. Again, fresh crabmeat makes the soup, so save this for coastal cooking.

2 T sweet butter
2 T flour
3 C milk
1 T Worcestershire sauce

½ t salt
Sprinkle of white pepper
1 lb fresh crabmeat
¼ C dry sherry

1. In a large saucepan over medium-low heat, melt the butter.
2. Whisk in the flour for 1 minute. Pour in the milk, whisking as it thickens for 2–3 minutes.
3. Add the Worcestershire sauce, salt, pepper, crabmeat, and sherry. Heat the soup to the simmering point.

Serves 4

SOUPS

CRAWDAD BISQUE

Most crayfish come from streams and lakes in the southern states and are shipped frozen and precooked to other parts of the country.

3 T sweet butter
2 – 2 ½ dozen crayfish
½ C onion, peeled and diced
½ C carrots, scraped and diced
½ C celeriac (celery root), peeled
   and diced
2 C fish stock
1 C water

½ C dry white vermouth (or dry
   white wine)
1 T cognac
4 peppercorns
⅔ C cooked rice
¼ C heavy cream
Salt

1. In a large soup pot over medium heat, melt the butter and sauté the whole crayfish, onion, carrots, and celeriac 5 minutes.
2. Add the fish stock, water, vermouth, cognac, and peppercorns. Bring the liquid to a boil (if crayfish are precooked and frozen, cook them 5 – 6 minutes; if fresh, cook them 2 – 3 minutes).
3. With a slotted spoon, remove the crayfish to a bowl.
4. Continue to simmer the stock over medium heat for 20 minutes.
5. Meanwhile, wearing gloves, remove and discard the heads of the crayfish. Shell the crayfish tails. Remove the black vein under the shell on the back of the crayfish tail.
6. Place the rinsed tails in a blender with the rice.
7. Strain the broth. Add 1 cup of broth to the blender. Purée with the crayfish and rice.
8. Place the crayfish purée in the soup pot with the remaining strained broth.
9. Heat well. Add the cream last and salt to taste. Do not boil the soup. Serve with croutons.

Serves 4

FISH

81

Finnan Haddie Chowder

The name is thought to be derived from Findhorn, Scotland. Finnan haddie is dried, salted, and smoked haddock. If the fish is highly salted, it should be covered with boiling water and drained before using in the chowder. This is a delicious soup to prepare when fresh fish isn't available.

½ C salt pork, diced
1 t olive oil
½ C onion, peeled and diced
1 C potatoes, peeled and diced
1 C water
½ lb finnan haddie, cut into bite-size pieces (skin removed)

2 C milk
Freshly ground black pepper
1 extra large egg, hard boiled
  and chopped
Sweet butter
Sprinkle of paprika

1. In a heavy skillet over high heat, render the salt pork in the oil 2–3 minutes. With a slotted spoon, remove the pieces and discard them.
2. Sauté the onion in the remaining fat. Cover and sweat for 5–8 minutes, letting the onion brown slightly.
3. In a saucepan over high heat, boil the potatoes in 1 cup water for 7–10 minutes.
4. Add the onion, finnan haddie, milk, and pepper. Cook for 20 minutes without boiling.
5. Before serving, add the chopped egg to the soup pot. Top each serving with a slice of butter and some paprika. Serve with oyster or soda crackers.

Serves 4

Fish Chowder

This chowder is mild and filling and a snap to prepare. Any fish fillet may be used, fresh or frozen. The larger pieces of fish may be broken into smaller pieces when it is served.

2 rashers lean bacon, diced
½ C onion, peeled and diced
2 parsley sprigs, de-stemmed and minced
1 C potatoes, peeled and diced
4 C cold water

½ t salt
Freshly ground black pepper
1 lb whitefish fillets (haddock, hake, or scrod)
1 C light cream

1. In a large pot over medium heat, sauté the bacon, onion, and parsley until the bacon is browned.
2. Add the potatoes, water, salt, and pepper.
3. Bring the water to a low boil and cook, covered, for 15 minutes.
4. Reduce to a simmer and uncover.
5. Add the fish and cream.
6. Simmer 5 minutes more. Do not boil.

Serves 4–6

FISH

FISH QUENELLES AND CELERY SOUP

These quenelles are firmer and easier to prepare than the classic style, but they're just as addictive. If you prefer larger quenelles, use tablespoons to form them.

3 C light fish stock
¼ C parsley, de-stemmed but
 uncut
½ C celery, cut in coarse strips
½ lb halibut steak
1 egg white
Dash of salt

Pinch of allspice
7 T heavy cream
Sweet butter for coating
Water
Finely chopped chives for gar-
 nish

1. Place the stock in a large saucepan and bring it to a boil. Add the parsley and celery, cover, and simmer for 20 minutes.
2. Meanwhile, trim the halibut of any skin and bone. Cut the halibut into small pieces. Place it in a food processor, and turn on and off in 2-second intervals three or four times.
3. Remove the ground halibut to a medium-size stainless steel mixing bowl placed in a larger bowl filled with ice. With a wooden spoon, mix the egg white into the halibut.
4. Stir in the salt and allspice.
5. Keeping the halibut mixture over the ice, blend in the cream 1 tablespoon at a time.
6. Butter the bottom of a large iron skillet.
7. To form the quenelles, wet a teaspoon with hot water, scoop it full of the mixture, and cap another teaspoon over it, shaping the mixture into a smooth oval.
8. With the top teaspoon, scrape the quenelle onto the skillet. Repeat for the rest of the mixture.
9. In a separate pot, heat water to the simmering point. Slowly pour the water down the inside of the skillet to avoid disturbing the quenelles. Add only enough water to the skillet so that the top parts of the quenelles are above the water.
10. Maintain the temperature at the simmering point. The quenelles should not be jostled by bubbling water. Cook 7 minutes. With a slotted spoon, turn over the quenelles and cook another 3 minutes.
11. Remove the quenelles with a slotted spoon to a plate.
12. Heat the stock to simmering. Ladle the stock into serving bowls. Add the quenelles to each serving and sprinkle with chives.

Serves 4–6

LOBSTER BISQUE

Have a special occasion coming up? This rich, delectable soup will be a favorite. The lobster should be boiled within a few hours of the time you plan to serve the soup so that it is exquisitely fresh.

1¼–1½ lb lobster
1 T dry sherry
1½ C fish stock
1½ C chicken stock
1 small celery stalk, with leaves
2 cloves
3 peppercorns
1 small bay leaf, crushed
1 C dry white wine

3 T sweet butter
1½ T flour
1 C milk
¾ C heavy cream
1 egg yolk, slightly beaten
Sprinkle of freshly ground nutmeg
¼ t salt
Sprinkle of white pepper

1. Remove all the lobster meat from the tail and claws. Shred it into small pieces. Place it in a bowl and douse it with sherry. Cover the bowl and set it aside.
2. Crush the shells with a mallet or lobster cracker (a nutcracker will do) and disjoint the legs, retaining all the juices for the lobster stock. The soft leg pieces may be ground in a meat grinder and added to the pot along with the fish stock, chicken stock, celery, cloves, peppercorns, bay leaf, and wine. (Omit the wine if it was used in your fish stock recipe.)
3. Cook all these ingredients at a low boil, uncovered, for 30 minutes. (Be sure to turn on the kitchen fan.)
4. Strain the lobster stock through a double layer of wet cheesecloth placed in a strainer over a bowl.
5. In a medium-size saucepan over medium heat, melt the butter and make a roux with the flour, whisking constantly. Add the milk and cook over medium-low heat while continuing to whisk. Do not boil.
6. Add 1½ cups of the lobster stock and the lobster meat to the milk mixture. Continue cooking the soup over low heat, stirring occasionally.
7. Meanwhile, mix the cream well with the egg yolk and add this to the bisque, making sure to whisk for 2–3 minutes as it heats to just below boiling.
8. Season with nutmeg, salt, and pepper to taste. The lobster will be salty, so taste the bisque before adding the salt.

Serves 4

MANHATTAN CLAM CHOWDER

New Englanders maintain that Manhattan Clam Chowder *is merely vegetable soup with clams. The Maine legislature once outlawed* Manhattan Clam Chowder, *saying it was a sacrilege to use tomatoes instead of milk. Nevertheless, this is a tasty and perfectly legal soup.*

20 cherrystone clams
2 C water
2 T olive oil
½ C salt pork, diced
½ C onion, peeled and diced
½ C sweet red bell pepper, cored, seeded, and diced
2 T parsley, de-stemmed and minced

2 C tomatoes, peeled and cored, with juice
½ C carrots, thinly sliced
½ t thyme
3 C water, with reserved clam juice
1 C potatoes, peeled and diced
½ t salt
Freshly ground black pepper

1. Scrub the clam shells with a wire brush. Place 1 cup of water in a steamer, the clams on a rack, cover, and steam the clams until the shells open slightly (about 4–7 minutes). Cool. Discard any clams that didn't open.
2. Over a bowl with a strainer on top, shuck the clams. Using a shucking or strong paring knife, place the clam in your hand (wear a glove or towel), slip the blade into one end of the shell, and pry it open. If the clam juice was lost in the steam water, strain it to use in the soup. Cut off the hard yellow clam muscle and discard it. Chop the rest of the clam, and reserve it for the chowder.
3. In a soup pot, heat the oil. Add the salt pork, and fry it over medium heat for 2–3 minutes. With a slotted spoon, discard the pork dice, retaining the oil and rendered fat.
4. Add the onion, red pepper, and parsley to the oil, and sauté it over medium heat for 5 minutes.
5. Add the tomatoes, carrots, thyme, and water mixed with reserved clam juice to equal 3 cups. Cover and cook the chowder at a low boil for 30 minutes.
6. Add the potatoes, and cook another 10–15 minutes. Season with salt and pepper.
7. Reduce the heat and add the clams. Simmer them 3–4 minutes.

Serves 4–6

MONKFISH ORANGE SOUP

The texture of monkfish is like lobster tail, and often it's referred to as a poor man's lobster. This soup combines Oriental flavors into an interesting appetizer. Keep adding the ingredients to the wok in quick succession so that the fish cooks 4–5 minutes at most.

1 T safflower oil
½ garlic clove, peeled, crushed, and minced
1 t onion, grated, with juice
1 t gingerroot, peeled and grated
¾ lb monkfish fillet, cut in ½-inch pieces
1 C navel orange (2 oranges), peeled and cut into ½-inch pieces

⅓ C cucumber, peeled and diced
1 ½ C fish stock (fumet)
⅔ C water
1 T cornstarch
⅛ t salt
1 T dry sherry
1 T sugar

1. Heat the oil in a wok or heavy skillet for frying. Stir-fry the garlic, onion, and grated gingerroot for a few seconds.
2. Add the monkfish and stir-fry it for 1 minute. The fish will turn white.
3. Add the orange and cucumber and stir once.
4. Pour in the fish stock, and bring it to a boil over high heat.
5. Meanwhile, in a measuring cup, mix the water with the cornstarch and add this mixture to the wok.
6. Boil the soup for 2–3 minutes until it clears and thickens.
7. Add the salt, sherry, and sugar. Stir once.

Serves 4

FISH

87

New England Bouillabaisse

Truly fresh fish is essential to a bouillabaisse, and if it means waiting on a dockside all the better. Once at a small French auberge in the Camargue on the Mediterranean, the innkeeper actually went out to catch the fish while we waited. The fresh catch made all the difference in the world. In this recipe we've tried to duplicate the style of that memorable bouillabaisse. This recipe is a guide. It may be adapted to any region of the country by substituting an appropriate range of seafood.

THE STOCK

¼ C olive oil
2 leeks (white part only), sliced
½ C onion, peeled and diced
3 garlic cloves, peeled and crushed
1 T parsley, de-stemmed and minced
1 T celery leaves, minced
3 C ripe tomatoes, cored and chopped
¼ t saffron threads
Bouquet garni (see right)
6 C water (or enough to cover the fish)

THE FISH (ALL OR A SELECTION OF THE FOLLOWING)

1 small whole red snapper (or sea bass), head, fins, and scales removed, cleaned
½ lb haddock (or cod)

1½ lb Maine lobster, parboiled 3 minutes, cracked and split
12 tinker mackerel, heads and fins removed, cleaned
1½ lb whole flounder, head and fins removed (or ocean perch fillets or skate wings)
8 blue mussels (or littleneck clams), scrubbed and steamed separately 4–5 minutes in dry white vermouth and water
Loaf of French bread, 1 or 2 days old
Parsley sprigs to garnish
Salt to taste

BOUQUET GARNI

¼ t anise seed
Orange rind strip
⅛ t rosemary
⅛ t thyme
3 peppercorns

1. Heat the olive oil in a very large soup pot over medium heat.
2. Add the leeks, onion, garlic, parsley, and celery. Cover and sweat 5–8 minutes.
3. Add the tomatoes and saffron. Cover and simmer 4 minutes.
4. Add the bouquet garni and 6 cups of water. Bring it to a low boil and simmer 15 minutes.
5. Strain the stock into a bowl, and return it to the rinsed soup pot. Discard the cooked vegetables and bouquet garni.
6. Bring the stock to a rolling boil, and place the whole snapper in the pot.
7. Break off the claws of the lobster, and leave the tail and head intact (unless it doesn't fit). Place all the lobster parts in the pot.

8. Add the more delicate fish (haddock or cod, small mackerel, flounder, perch) last. If the water doesn't cover, add more, although the less water the stronger the broth. Press the fish into the broth with a slotted spoon. Cook at a low boil another 6–8 minutes.
9. Meanwhile, steam the mussels or clams separately until they open.
10. Cut the French bread in rounds ½-inch thick. Dry the bread in a low oven if necessary, but don't toast it.
11. Carefully remove the fish with a slotted spoon to a large, warmed platter, placing the whole fish in the center and the shellfish and smaller fish around it. Garnish with parsley sprigs.
12. Place a few slices of bread in each flat soup plate.
13. Taste for salt, which may not be needed if the lobster was boiled in saltwater. Pour the broth into a soup tureen.
14. At the table, ladle some broth over the bread, and let guests choose the shellfish and fish they wish.

Serves 4–6

ॐ
NEW ENGLAND CLAM CHOWDER

This is a basic chowder found on many restaurant menus across the country. Once you've tasted a seashore fresh bowl of chowder, you'll forget the canned variety.

½ C salt pork, diced
1 t olive oil
½ C onion, peeled and diced
2 C potatoes, peeled and diced
2 C clam juice (2 dozen shucked cherrystone clams yield approximately 2 cups of juice)
1½ C cold water
1 C clams, minced (2 dozen

shucked cherrystone clams yield approximately 1 cup)
(see *Manhattan Clam Chowder* on p. 86 for instructions on how to shuck clams)
1 C half-and-half
½ t salt
Sprinkle of white pepper
2 T sweet butter

1. In a large saucepan, sauté the salt pork in the oil over medium-high heat. When about a tablespoon of fat is rendered, remove the pork pieces with a slotted spoon and discard them.
2. Sauté the onion in the oil for 2–3 minutes.
3. Add the potatoes, clam juice, and water.
4. Boil them over medium heat, and simmer for 7–10 minutes.
5. Add the clams and half-and-half, and heat the chowder to scalding. Do not boil.
6. Add the salt and pepper.

7. Ladle clams and potatoes into each bowl, and add the milk broth. Float a dab of butter on the top of each, and serve with a bowl of oyster crackers and a cruet of dry sherry on the table.

Serves 6

&

OYSTER BISQUE

This bisque takes no longer than 5 minutes to prepare — after the oysters are shucked. The bisque makes a convenient supper or an elegant, spontaneous after-theater get-together.

1½ dozen oysters	1 t Worcestershire sauce
2 T sweet butter	½ C heavy cream
⅛ t paprika	2 C milk

1. Scrub the oyster shells with a wire brush. Over a bowl with a strainer on top, shuck the oysters. Using a shucking or strong paring knife, place the oyster in your hand (wear a glove or towel), slip the blade into the hinge at the side, and pry it open. Reserve the liquor along with the oyster. Discard the shells.
2. Over medium heat in a saucepan, melt the butter. Add the paprika and Worcestershire sauce.
3. Add the oysters with their liquor to the butter until the edges of the oysters curl (about 2 minutes).
4. Remove 2 of the oysters with a slotted spoon, and place them in a blender with the cream. Blend 1 minute.
5. Add this mixture and the milk to the oysters in the pan. Heat to below boiling.
6. Make sure each serving has 4 whole oysters.

Serves 4

SOUPS

RED SNAPPER CREOLE SOUP

Except for parsley, this is a red soup. Related to sea bass, red snapper is known as "the king of fish" in New Orleans. It is usually stuffed and served whole. Snapper is somewhat difficult to fillet, so we suggest you buy 2 – 2½-lb whole snapper and have the fishmonger fillet it for you (saving the head and parts to make stock).

3 T safflower oil
1 garlic clove, peeled, crushed,
   and minced
1 C onion, peeled and diced
1 C celery, threaded and diced
¼ C sweet red bell pepper,
   cored, seeded, and diced
1 T parsley, de-stemmed and
   minced
3 C tomatoes, peeled and cored,
   with juice

½ t chile powder (or 2 – 3 drops
   Tabasco sauce)
½ t paprika
⅛ t allspice
3 C fish stock (or 1 C clam juice
   and 2 C stock)
¼ C dry red wine
¼ t salt
1½ lb red snapper, filleted and
   cut into pieces
4 lemon slices

1. In a large soup pot (enameled is better for fish), heat the oil over medium-high heat.
2. Sauté the garlic, onion, celery, sweet red pepper, and parsley 5 minutes.
3. Cover the vegetables, and let them sweat over low heat for 10 minutes.
4. Add the tomatoes, chile powder, paprika, allspice, fish stock, and wine.
5. Cover and simmer the soup for 30 minutes. Add salt to taste.
6. Add the snapper pieces, and simmer for 5 minutes. The fish should turn white.
7. Ladle some fish and broth into each bowl. Place a lemon slice on top as a garnish.

Serves 4

FISH

91

SCALLOP HOMINY CHOWDER

Prepared hominy comes in white and yellow kernels. For pleasing eye and taste appeal, cut the potatoes and scallops to match the size of the kernels.

4 C water
2 C celery, diced (including the leaves)
⅔ C leeks (white part only), diced
3 T sweet butter
2 C potatoes, peeled and diced

1 C prepared hominy
½ lb scallops, cut hominy-size
½ C milk
¼ C heavy cream
½ t salt
Sprinkle of paprika

1. In a large saucepan over high heat, bring the water to a boil, and cook the celery in it for 10 minutes. Drain, reserving the liquid. Discard the celery. Return the celery water to the rinsed pan.
2. In a heavy skillet, sauté the leeks in the butter 2–3 minutes. Cover and sweat the leeks over medium heat for 5 minutes. Add the leeks and potatoes to the celery water.
3. Cook them covered for 10 minutes.
4. Add the hominy.
5. Add the scallops and simmer. The scallops are done when you cut them and they're opaque (about 1–2 minutes — don't overcook).
6. Immediately, stir in the milk, cream, and salt. Heat but do not boil.
7. Ladle the chowder into bowls, and serve with a sprinkle of paprika.

Serves 4–6

SHRIMP BISQUE (CHILLED)

Fast and delectable. Double or triple the recipe, and ladle Shrimp Bisque from a large glass bowl as an elegant appetizer for lawn parties and luncheons.

½ lb fresh shrimp
1 C boiling water
½ C cucumber, peeled, seeded, and finely grated
1 t chives, minced

½ t paprika
½ t salt
½ t prepared mustard
4 C cultured buttermilk

1. Steam the shrimp over the boiling water for 3 minutes — until they turn bright pink. Remove the shells (and the veins, if the fish market hasn't already done so).
2. In a mixing bowl, combine the cucumber, chives, paprika, salt, mustard, and buttermilk.
3. Add the shrimp.
4. Stir well and chill 2 hours before serving.

Serves 4

&ᴏ

SKATE WING AND
COCONUT SOUP

The crunchy texture of the coconut meat and the delicate taste of skate wing makes this an intriguing Oriental-style soup. Skate is considered a trash fish by some but has a mild flavor and texture similar to sole.

2 ½ C fish stock
⅔ C fresh coconut milk (see
   Coco Loco Soup on p. 190 on
   how to prepare coconut milk)
½ C fresh finely grated coconut
   meat

¼ t salt
2 T sweet butter
½ lb skate wing, cut bite-size
2 scallions, sliced

1. Place the stock, coconut milk, coconut meat, and salt in a large saucepan. Bring the liquid to a low boil.
2. In an iron skillet over medium heat, melt the butter. Sauté the skate wing only until opaque (about 1 – 2 minutes).
3. Transfer the skate wing to the broth and warm briefly.
4. Ladle into individual bowls. Sprinkle on the scallions.

Serves 4

FISH

❧

SMOKED MUSSEL BILLI-BI

Billi-bi (Billy-by) was created by a chef at Ciro's in Paris in 1925 and was named after a customer who preferred the mussel broth to the mussels. Now the mussels usually are either blended back into the soup or added just before serving. Smoked mussels aren't a traditional ingredient, but they add a fireside taste and aroma.

3 T sweet butter
1 C leeks (white part only, well washed and thinly sliced)
2 t parsley, de-stemmed and minced
¼ t thyme
1 ½ dozen mussels, well scrubbed

2 C vinho verde (young Portuguese white wine)
1 C water
Cheesecloth
Smoked tinned mussels (3.66 oz), well drained
1 C heavy cream

1. Melt the butter in a saucepan over medium-low heat.
2. Add the leeks, parsley, and thyme.
3. Cover them, and let them sweat over low heat for 5 minutes.
4. Make sure the mussels are fresh and well scrubbed with a stiff brush. Discard any open mussels. Squeeze the shell. If it opens even a crack, throw it away. Trim off the beard (threadlike material) with scissors.
5. Place the mussels in a large soup pot with the wine and water. Add the cooked leeks and herbs.
6. Bring the liquid to a boil over high heat. Turn the heat to medium, cover the pot, and boil for 8 minutes.
7. Now the inverse rule applies. Any mussels that *did not* open should be discarded. This is a sure sign they shouldn't be eaten.
8. Drain the mussel stock through a double layer of wet cheesecloth placed in a strainer over a bowl.
9. Pick the fresh mussel meat from the shells, and add it to the strained stock. Discard the shells.
10. Spread the smoked mussels on paper towels to drain off the oil.
11. Add the smoked mussels and heavy cream to the stock and fresh mussels.
12. Return these ingredients to a large saucepan, and heat them to the boiling point. Ladle fresh and smoked mussels into each dish. Pour the broth over the mussels.

Serves 4

SOLE SOUP MARSEILLES

This soup melds the Mediterranean tastes of bouillabaisse with much less preparation. Orzo is a rice-shaped pasta that lends a thick consistency. Technically, sole is a small flounder often imported under the name Dover or lemon sole. Flounder, or fluke, often is called sole in this country.

2 T olive oil
½ C leeks (white part only), well washed and sliced
½ C onion, peeled and diced
3 small garlic cloves, peeled, crushed, and minced
6¼ C water
1 C tomatoes, peeled, cored, and chopped
1 lb sole fillet, cut in large pieces
1 large pinch saffron threads
½ C orzo
1½ T cognac
1½ t salt
Sprinkle of white pepper

1. Heat the oil in a large soup pot over medium heat. Add the leeks, onion, and garlic. Cover and sweat them for 5–8 minutes, stirring occasionally.
2. Add 6 cups of water, the tomatoes, and sole. Bring the liquid to a boil. Cook the sole and tomatoes approximately 8–10 minutes.
3. Meanwhile, in a small saucepan, briefly boil the saffron threads in remaining ¼ cup water. Pour them into the soup.
4. Cool the soup and blend it (in the blender) in batches until it is well puréed.
5. Return the soup to the rinsed pot, and bring it to a boil. Add the orzo, and cook until it is soft (about 15 minutes).
6. Add the cognac, salt, and white pepper.

Serves 6–8

FISH
95

&

SPANISH GARLIC FISH SOUP

Aioli is used on potatoes in the south of France. This recipe comes from the Spanish island of Minorca and the port of Mahon from whence mayonnaise derives its name. Homemade aioli will not be as thick as prepared mayonnaise, but it blends much better into the soup. Bread crumbs are a cinch to make. Simply process crusts or old bread in a blender or food processor, and freeze them for use as needed.

1½ C bread crumbs
4 C water
1 C potatoes, peeled and thinly
   sliced
2 T olive oil
½ lb hake
½ t salt
Sprinkle of white pepper

AIOLI (GARLIC MAYONNAISE)

1 egg yolk
1 t water
1 medium-size garlic clove,
   peeled, crushed, and minced
⅛ t salt
½ C olive oil

1. Place the bread crumbs in a medium-size soup pot. Add the water and, as the mixture boils over medium-high heat, stir well for 2–3 minutes.
2. Add the potatoes, and continue to boil 10–15 minutes.
3. Meanwhile, in a heavy iron skillet, heat 2 tablespoons of olive oil. Cut the hake into 2 pieces, and sauté them 1 minute on each side in the oil.
4. Remove the fish with a spatula to the soup pot.
5. Add salt and pepper. Simmer the soup, covered, for 20 minutes.
6. To make the aioli: place the egg yolk, water, garlic, and salt in a blender. Slowly add the oil in a thin stream as you purée the yolk. (Prepared mayonnaise may be used. Simply blend minced garlic into ½ cup of mayonnaise.)
7. Remove the soup from the burner. Stir well, and let it cool slightly. Add the aioli to the soup, stirring so the egg mixture blends completely.
8. Heat and simmer a few minutes to blend the flavors.

Serves 4

VIETNAMESE SWEET AND SOUR FISH SOUP

A deep golden color, this flavorful soup combines ordinary ingredients into an exotic blend. This makes an excellent prelude to your favorite stir-fry.

2 T peanut oil
½ C onion, peeled and diced
1 garlic clove, peeled, crushed, and minced
3 scallions (white part and 1 inch of green stalk), sliced
4 C water
4–5 drops hot pepper sauce
Grated rind of 1 lemon

2 star anise seeds
¼ t saffron threads
2 T rice wine vinegar
1 T lemongrass in a bouquet garni
1 T (scant) honey
⅔ C pineapple, small chunks
½ lb hake, cut in ½-inch chunks
1 T cornstarch
1 T tamari soy sauce

1. In a large saucepan, heat the oil and sauté the onion, garlic, and scallions briefly. Cover and sweat them for 5–8 minutes.
2. Add the water, pepper sauce, lemon rind, star anise, saffron threads, vinegar, lemongrass, and honey. Bring them to a boil, cover, and simmer for 15 minutes.
3. Add the pineapple and hake. Simmer for 10 minutes or until the hake is opaque.
4. In a cup or bowl, mix the cornstarch in the soy sauce and stir the mixture into the soup. Bring the soup to the simmering point until it thickens and clears (2–3 minutes).

Serves 4–6

FISH

WING OF LOX SOUP

Most fish markets dispense with the fins (wings), tails, and backbones of fresh salmon and smoked lox. But you may ask the fishmonger to save them for you. This soup has fish bones. Place a plate on the table as a reminder. Various vegetables may be substituted.

2 lbs wing of lox
6 C water
1 C potatoes, peeled and coarsely chopped
1 C carrots, scraped and cut into 1-inch pieces
1 C celery, threaded and cut into

1-inch pieces (including the leaves)
½ C onion, peeled and coarsely chopped
½ t salt
Freshly ground black pepper
Sour cream

1. Rinse off the lox or fresh salmon. Discard the head or freeze it for making stock. Place the salmon in a large soup pot and add the water. Bring it to a boil over high heat. Lower the heat, cover, and simmer the stock for 30 minutes.
2. Prepare the vegetables. Add them to the soup pot. Cook at a low boil for 30 minutes.
3. Taste the soup for salt. Smoked lox usually is heavily salted; fresh salmon is not. Start with ½ teaspoon salt for fresh salmon, and add more if necessary. Pepper to taste.
4. Make sure that each person is served a few pieces of salmon and some of each vegetable. Remind diners to watch for fish bones.
5. Place a small bowl of sour cream on the table as a topping.

Serves 4

SOUPS

MEAT

Basic Beef Stock 101
Basic Brown Veal Stock 102

SOUPS
100

Basic Beef Stock

Searing the meat until it is dark brown will produce a darker stock; however, browning the meat seals in some of the juices. This is the reason that only half of the meat is browned. Pour in $\frac{1}{4}$ cup dry red wine at the beginning of cooking time, if you have it on hand.

4 T olive oil
2 lbs stewing beef
1 lb beef marrow bones
2 small carrots
2 small celery stalks
2 small onions, peeled and halved

1 bay leaf
4 parsley sprigs
6 black peppercorns
10 C cold water
1 t salt

1. Heat the oil in a heavy skillet over high heat. Brown half the meat.
2. With a slotted spoon, remove the browned meat and place it in a soup pot. Except the water and salt, add all the other ingredients, including the other half of the meat.
3. Pour 1 cup of water into the skillet, and scrape the bottom with a spoon to remove the browned meat juices. Pour this into the soup pot. Add the remaining 9 cups of water.
4. Bring the water to a boil. Reduce the heat and partially cover. Boil over low heat for 1 ½ hours.
5. Add the salt.
6. Strain the stock into a large bowl, and reserve the meat and vegetables for other uses. Cool the stock. Skim off any fat, and pour the stock through a double layer of wet cheesecloth placed in a strainer over a large bowl.

Yields approximately 7 cups

Meat

BASIC BROWN VEAL STOCK

This is a rich, tasty stock that freezes well. It may be kept in the refrigerator 3 – 4 days, although then it must be boiled before using.

2 ½ lbs veal bones
2 C carrots, scraped and cut into
   rounds
1 C onion, peeled and chopped
2 garlic cloves, peeled, crushed,
   and minced

2 T parsley, chopped with stems
   (about 6 sprigs)
¼ t dried thyme (or a few fresh
   sprigs)
2 T tomato paste
2 T water
12 C water

1. Heat the oven to 400° F. Place the veal bones in a shallow ovenproof pan, and roast the bones until they are caramel colored (about 45 – 60 minutes).
2. Meanwhile, place the carrots, onion, garlic, parsley, and thyme in a stockpot or heavy Dutch oven.
3. Mix the tomato paste with 2 tablespoons water, and add it to the vegetables.
4. Turn the heat to high, add the browned bones, and sweat the vegetables, covered, for 10 minutes, stirring occasionally.
5. Add 1 cup of water. Boil over high heat, reducing the liquid by half to a thick glaze. Repeat with another cup of water. The darker the thick liquid the better.
6. Add the remaining 10 cups of water and simmer the stock, covered, for 1 hour. Remove the bones. Strain out the vegetables and discard them.
7. Cool. Strain the stock through a double layer of wet cheesecloth placed in a strainer over a large bowl.
8. Refrigerate overnight. Skim any solidified fat from the top.

Yields approximately 10 cups

BAJA GAZPACHO (CHILLED)

Gazpacho has become a summer favorite from coast to coast, and avocado gives this version a distinct California identity. If there's not enough time to chill the soup, add an ice cube to each serving.

3 C light consommé (1 ½ C water can be added to double-strength consommé to dilute it)
½ C cucumber, peeled, seeded, and diced
½ C tomatos, peeled, cored, and diced

½ C avocado, peeled, seeded, and diced
⅓ C small shrimp, cooked, peeled, and de-veined
2 T red wine vinegar
1 T olive oil
1 T onion, peeled and grated (with juice)
½ t Worcestershire sauce

1. Place the consommé in a bowl or casserole that has a cover.
2. Add all the ingredients to the consommé, and chill it, covered, for at least 2 hours. Stir before serving.

Serves 4

BEEF BARLEY SOUP

The barley doubles in volume as it absorbs the stock. Be sure to taste for salt before adding more. This hearty, no-nonsense soup has a refreshing simplicity to it.

3 T olive oil
1 lb lean stewing beef, cut bite-size
7 C beef or brown veal stock
½ C pearl barley
1 T molasses
1 large garlic clove, peeled and diced

¼ C parsley, de-stemmed and minced
¼ t thyme
½ C onion, peeled and diced
1 t salt
Freshly ground black pepper

1. Heat the oil in a large Dutch oven or soup pot. Add the beef, and sauté it for 5–7 minutes.
2. Add the stock, barley, molasses, garlic, parsley, thyme, and onion. Bring the soup to a boil, cover, and simmer it about 1 hour until the barley is tender. Add more stock if necessary.
3. Add the salt and pepper to taste.

Serves 6

MEAT

103

BEEF CRANBERRY SOUP

Meat has been paired with tart fruits since medieval cookery. The combination in this case is spectacular.

½ lb lean stewing beef, cut bite-size
2 T sweet butter
1 T olive oil
⅓ C onion, peeled and diced
1 garlic clove, peeled and minced
½ C mushrooms, de-stemmed, peeled (not washed), and thinly sliced
1 T parsley, de-stemmed and minced

¼ t fresh tarragon leaves, minced
2 C beef stock
1 C water
1 C cranberry juice
1 C cranberries
1 T sugar
1 T tomato paste
1 C flat wide noodles
¾ t salt
Freshly ground black pepper
¼ C sour cream

1. In a Dutch oven over high heat, brown the beef. Remove the beef with a slotted spoon and set it aside.
2. Reduce the heat to medium-low, and melt the butter and oil. Briefly sauté the onion, garlic, and mushrooms. Cover and sweat the vegetables for 10 minutes, stirring occasionally, until the mushrooms are soft.
3. Add the parsley, tarragon, stock, water, cranberry juice and berries, sugar, tomato paste, and browned beef. Bring the soup to a boil, cover, and simmer for 45 minutes.
4. Meanwhile, toward the end of the simmering time, cook the noodles in a separate pot according to package directions. Drain the noodles, and add them to the soup. Season with salt and pepper to taste.
5. Add a spoonful of sour cream to each serving.

Serves 4–6

SOUPS

Beef Espresso Consommé

This clear, dark, distinctive consommé is an elegant appetizer or light refreshment. The browning of the meat and the coffee enhances the rich brown color and taste. If you haven't clarified a consommé, try it and witness the magic firsthand.

2 T olive oil
1 lb stewing beef
1 small onion, peeled and quartered
½ lb beef marrow bones
¾ lb shank veal cutlets (with bone in)
3 peppercorns
1 clove

12 C water
1 celery stalk with leaves, chopped
1 parsley sprig
1 small carrot, chopped
⅔ C espresso coffee, freshly brewed
1 t salt
1 egg white and shell

1. In a large skillet, heat the oil.
2. Over high heat, brown the stewing beef and onion until both are very dark (on the verge of burnt).
3. Place the marrow bones, veal, peppercorns, clove, browned beef, and onion in a large Dutch oven or heavy soup pot and add the water. Slowly bring it to a boil. (The slower this process the more juices are extracted from the meat.)
4. Add the celery, parsley, and carrot.
5. During the first 30 minutes, skim off the fat and scum.
6. Cover the stock, and simmer at a low boil for not less than 3 hours.
7. Place a double thick layer of wet cheesecloth in a strainer and pour the stock through. Retain the meats for a stew or main course later.
8. Add the coffee. Stir in the salt to taste.
9. Refrigerate several hours, and remove the fat that congeals on top.
10. To clarify the consommé: place 1 egg white and crushed eggshell in 1 quart of cold consommé.
11. Bring the consommé to a boil, beating constantly with a whisk. Simmer, covered, for 30 minutes. Skim off any foam or scum.
12. Strain the consommé through a strainer lined with a double layer of wet cheesecloth.

Serves 8–12

Meat

105

BLACK-EYED PEA SOUP

*Southerners traditionally serve black-eyed peas (also known as cow peas)
on New Year's Day. Alabamans throw a sterilized silver dollar into the
soup tureen for good luck. Black-eyed peas, contrary to their name, are a
bean. With the addition of brown rice, this soup provides a filling and nutritious meal.*

2 C dried black-eyed peas
10 C water
1 lb smoked ham hock, leftover
  ham bone, or smoked ham roll
½ C celery, threaded and diced
¼ C onion, peeled and diced
2 T parsley, de-stemmed and
  minced

1 garlic clove, peeled, crushed,
  and minced
¼ t cayenne
1 t salt
1 C cooked brown rice
Tomato relish (optional)

1. In a large soup pot over high heat, bring the peas to a boil in 4 cups of
   water for 5 minutes. Cover the pot and turn off the burner. Leave the
   peas for 2 hours (or overnight) without removing the lid. This precooks
   the peas.
2. Add the ham hock, celery, onion, parsley, garlic, cayenne, salt, and the
   remaining 6 cups of water to the peas in the pot.
3. Bring the soup to a boil. Cover and reduce the heat. Let the soup simmer for 1 ½ hours, stirring occasionally.
4. Remove the ham hock, and cut the meat from the bone into bite-size
   pieces. Return the ham meat to the pot, discarding the bone.
5. Taste for salt; add more if necessary.
6. Add more water if too much has boiled away. Add the cooked rice, and
   heat the soup thoroughly.
7. Place a bowl of tomato relish on the table as a garnish.

Serves 4–6

SOUPS

BLUE CHEESE SOUP

More blue cheese may be served in a bowl on the table. The flavor of this soup is mild, creamy, and appetizing.

1 lb stewing beef
8 C water
1 T fresh basil leaves, minced
1 T parsley, de-stemmed and
  minced

1 ½ C cooked homemade or commercial flat egg noodles
¾ t salt
Freshly ground black pepper
2 oz blue or Roquefort cheese

1. Place the stewing meat in a large pot, cover it with the water, and bring it to a boil.
2. Add the basil and parsley.
3. Lower the heat and cook, covered, at a low boil for 3 hours. Stir occasionally.
4. Cook the noodles separately according to package directions. Drain and add them to the beef soup.
5. Add the salt and pepper to taste.
6. Break up the blue cheese and stir it into the soup. Cook the cheese only until it melts. Do not boil the soup.

Serves 8

BORSCHT (CHILLED)

The magenta of garden-fresh beets, the yellow rounds of the eggs, and the crisp green tinge of cucumber are not only vivid in color but taste as well. Beet greens can be saved, washed, and cooked down with diced bacon and a little oil and vinegar.

4–5 medium-size beets
Water to cover
2 ½ C beet liquid (from above)
1 C beef stock
1 T onion, peeled and grated

1 T fresh lemon juice
½ t salt
8 thin slices cucumber, peeled
2 hard-boiled eggs, sliced
¼ C sour cream

1. Scrub the beets, and cut the stems no shorter than 1 inch from the top. Place them in a large saucepan. Add water to cover.
2. Bring the water to a boil, and cook the beets approximately 45 minutes. Test with a knife to see if they're tender.

3. Drain the beets, reserving the beet water. Place the beets in cold water, and slip off the skins by hand. Chop the beets.
4. Add the beet liquid to the beef stock.
5. In a blender, blend 1 cup of beets with ½ cup of beef-beet liquid.
6. Combine the blended beets with the remaining beef-beet liquid. Add the onion, lemon juice, and salt to taste.
7. Chill at least 2 hours.
8. Stir the borscht well before pouring it into serving bowls.
9. Float 2 cucumber slices and egg slices on top of each serving, and crown with a dollop of sour cream.

Serves 4

๛

CHAMPAGNE AND BRIE
ONION SOUP

A special occasion will be even more special with this soup to start the evening. Contrary to what one might think, brut champagne is drier than extra dry.

3 C onion, peeled and thinly sliced
3 T sweet butter
4 C beef stock

1 ½ C brut champagne
6 T brie, at room temperature
Freshly ground black pepper

1. In a heavy soup pot over medium heat, sauté the onion in the butter. Stir, cover, and sweat for 7 minutes.
2. Remove the cover and add the beef stock. Cover and simmer the soup 20 minutes.
3. Uncork the champagne, and reserve 1 ½ cups for the soup. Pour the remaining champagne for guests.
4. Trim the crust from the brie. The cheese should be soft and runny.
5. Add the champagne and brie to the soup. Simmer 3 minutes more, and stir until the cheese is blended into the stock.
6. Serve with French bread.

Serves 4

CHICK-PEA WITH DITALINI

By passing the soup through a food mill instead of liquefying it, a more interesting texture remains for this country noontime soup. Ditalini (little fingers) are half-inch-long tube pasta. Other pastas, of course, may be substituted.

2 rashers lean bacon
½ C onion, peeled and chopped
1 garlic clove, peeled, crushed, and minced
2 C prepared chick-peas, with juice (19-oz can)
1 C water

½ C tomatoes, peeled, cored, and chopped
1 T parsley, de-stemmed and minced
¼ t fresh tarragon leaves, minced
¼ C ditalini

1. In a large saucepan, fry the bacon. Remove the bacon with a slotted spoon, cool slightly, and break it into bits. Set the bacon bits aside.
2. Over medium heat, sauté the onion and garlic in the bacon fat for 2–3 minutes.
3. Add the chick-peas, water, tomatoes, parsley, tarragon, and bacon bits. Cook, covered, for 15 minutes.
4. Meanwhile, cook the ditalini in a separate pot according to directions.
5. Pass the entire contents of the chick-pea mixture through a food mill with a medium-fine disc. Return the processed mixture to the rinsed saucepan.
6. Add the drained ditalini and heat.

Serves 4

MEAT

109

CHILE PUMPKIN SOUP

Jicama (hee-ka-ma) is a mild, sweet, turnip-shaped bulb. It's good sliced thinly, sprinkled with lime juice, and eaten raw. In this southwestern-style soup, the jicama provides a slightly crunchy texture.

2 T onion, peeled and diced
3 T corn oil
2 jalapeño peppers, de-stemmed, de-seeded, and minced
3 T parsley, de-stemmed and minced
½ t cumin
1 C jicama, peeled and diced

2 C beef stock
1 C water
2 C fresh sugar pumpkin, peeled, diced, cooked, and puréed (if unavailable, use canned pumpkin)
¾ t salt

1. In a heavy soup pot over medium heat, sauté the onion in the oil 5 minutes.
2. Add the jalapeño peppers, parsley, cumin, and jicama. Continue sautéeing for 3 minutes. Cover and sweat the vegetables 5 – 8 minutes until the jicama is soft.
3. Add the stock, water, and pumpkin. Bring the soup to a boil. Cover and simmer it for 20 minutes. Add the salt to taste.

Serves 4 – 6

CHINESE STUFFED MUSHROOM SOUP

This is an elegant Oriental soup. Use the best available pork, fresh spinach, and white, fresh mushrooms. Make sure to steam the pork the full 20 minutes. If it looks pinkish, add a few more minutes to the cooking time. This recipe may be prepared with beef or chicken stock.

2 center-cut pork chops
½ C spinach leaves, de-stemmed, washed, and finely sliced
2 T scallions, minced
¼ C water chestnuts, drained and diced
1 t soy sauce

1 T chicken stock
1 T cornstarch
⅛ t ground ginger
8 medium-size mushroom caps, de-stemmed and peeled
4 C beef stock

1. Cut away the fat and bone from the chops. Place the pork meat in a meat grinder and grind it.
2. Place the ground pork in a bowl. Add the spinach, scallions, and water chestnuts.

3. In a separate small bowl, mix the soy sauce, chicken stock, cornstarch, and ginger.
4. Add this mixture to the meat and blend well.
5. Trim around the mushroom gills so the cap is more open.
6. Divide the filling into 8 portions, and stuff each of the mushroom caps.
7. Place the caps in a vegetable steamer, cover, and steam them for 20 minutes.
8. Meanwhile, heat the beef stock.
9. Place 2 mushrooms filling side up in each shallow serving bowl, and ladle the broth around the mushrooms.

Serves 4

&

CHINESE VEGETABLE SOUP

Stir-frying is fast and keeps the vegetables fresh and tender without cooking all the nutrients out of them. For a garnish, sprinkle fried noodles, chopped peanuts, or crushed rice cakes on each serving.

½ C mushroom caps, peeled and sliced
1 C bok choy, finely sliced
1 C broccoli, divided into small spears
1 C snow peas, tips removed and sliced on the diagonal
½ C mung bean sprouts
½ C pickled baby corn cobs
⅓ C safflower oil
½ t sesame seed oil

1 garlic clove, peeled, crushed, and minced
½ t fresh gingerroot, peeled and grated
3 scallions, roots and 1 inch of greens, thinly sliced
3 C beef stock
2½ C water
3 T cornstarch
1 T soy sauce

1. Prepare all the vegetables and set them aside.
2. In a wok (or large heavy iron skillet), heat the oils and add the garlic, gingerroot, and scallions. Stir-fry 1 minute with a slotted spoon.
3. Add the vegetables one at a time. Stir-fry each vegetable for 1 minute before adding the next one.
4. Cover and steam for 3 minutes.
5. Add the stock and 2 cups of water. Bring the soup to a boil.
6. In a measuring cup, mix remaining ½ cup of water with the cornstarch, and add this mixture to the soup.
7. Add the soy sauce, and stir until the soup thickens.

Serves 6

CHINESE WATERCRESS SOUP

If the beef stock is concentrated, dilute it with water to make 4 cups. A bunch of watercress usually yields 1 cup, fully packed. Run your fingers along the stems to remove the leaves. Surprise diners with a poetic Chinese name such as Celestial Soup or Moondrop Delight.

2 T safflower oil
¼ C bamboo shoots, drained and finely sliced
3 scallions, roots and 4 inches of greens, sliced into ½-inch rounds
1 C watercress, washed and de-stemmed

4 C beef stock
1 t rice wine (or rice vinegar)
2 t soy sauce
2 T water
¼ t safflower oil
1 T cornstarch
1 egg, slightly beaten

1. Heat the oil in a wok or large saucepan over medium-high heat. Sauté the bamboo shoots and scallions for 3 minutes.
2. Add the watercress and stir-fry for 1–2 minutes. After the watercress wilts, add the beef stock, rice wine, and soy sauce. Bring the soup to a boil.
3. In a measuring cup, mix the water with the oil and cornstarch, and pour the mixture into the soup, stirring 2–3 minutes, until the soup clears and thickens.
4. Pour the beaten egg into the soup, breaking it with a fork to separate the egg into fine shreds.

Serves 4

SOUPS

CHLODNIK (CHILLED)

Chlodnik (shlud-nick) is a cold, soured, uncooked borscht made in the old country with fermented beet juice. Although served cold, chlodnik isn't a light summer soup but a substantial meal combining a salad (garnishes) with the soup (borscht) and, in this version, the veal as well.

1 lb beets, well scrubbed
Water to cover
5 C beet greens, well washed, de-stemmed, and coarsely chopped
¼ C fresh dill, de-stemmed and minced
½ C dill pickle juice
1 t sugar
1 ½ C veal stock (see below)

VEAL STOCK

2 lbs veal shanks
12 C cold water
1 C onion, peeled and diced
1 C carrots, scraped and diced

1 C celery, threaded and diced
8 black peppercorns, crushed and tied in cheesecloth

GARNISHES

1 C cooked veal, cut into bite-size pieces off the shank bones
2 hard-boiled eggs, peeled and sliced
½ lb crayfish tails, cooked, peeled, and de-veined (shrimp may be substituted)
1 C sour cream
1 C cucumber, peeled, seeded, and diced

1. Leave 1 inch of the stem on the beets so that they don't bleed as much when cooking. Boil them in water to cover until they are tender (approximately 20 minutes).
2. Reserve 2 cups of the cooking water from the beets.
3. Place the beets under cold running water, and slip off the skins and stems with your fingers.
4. Place the cooked beets and greens in a large soup pot. Cover them, and cook the greens over low heat until they wilt (approximately 5–7 minutes). Stir them occasionally so they don't burn and stick. Add a little of the cooking water from the beets if necessary.
5. In a blender or food processor, purée the beets, greens, and dill with 2 cups of cooking water from the beets.
6. Add the dill pickle juice and sugar to the beet mixture, and stir in well.
7. To make the veal stock, place the veal shanks in 12 cups of water with the onion, carrots, celery, and peppercorns. Bring them to a boil, and remove any foam with a slotted spoon. Simmer the stock, covered, for 1 hour.
8. Remove the veal shanks to a separate bowl to cool.
9. Strain off 1 ½ cups of the veal stock, and reserve the remaining stock and vegetables for other recipes.

10. Add the 1 ½ cups of veal stock to the beet chlodnik, and refrigerate it for 3–4 hours or until it is well chilled.
11. Place the garnishes in serving bowls, or arrange them on a serving platter at the center of the table. White bowls best offset the brilliant beet color.

Serves 4

&

COCK-A-LEEKIE SOUP

Medieval cookbooks often combine fruits and stocks. This Scottish recipe is an old castle favorite with the addition of the leek introduced to Scotland by the French.

8 C brown veal stock
1 lb chicken pieces (leg plus
   thigh)
1 small carrot
1 small celery stalk
1 small onion

1 t salt
Sprinkle of white pepper
2 C leeks (white part only),
   thinly sliced
8 prunes, cooked, pitted, and
   halved
8 dried apricots, cooked

1. In a large soup pot or Dutch oven over medium heat, bring the veal stock, chicken, carrot, celery, and onion to a boil.
2. Cook, covered, at a low boil for 1 hour.
3. Strain out the vegetables and chicken, reserving the stock.
4. Let the chicken cool. Remove and discard the skin and bones, and cut the chicken meat into bite-size pieces.
5. Skim the fat from the stock.
6. Return the chicken meat and stock to the pot. Salt and pepper to taste.
7. Add the leeks to the soup, and boil for 7–10 minutes until they are soft.
8. The prunes and apricots may be added to the soup in the kitchen or passed around at the table. (To prepare them, soak overnight. Bring them to a boil for 10 minutes until they're soft.)

Serves 4–6

SOUPS

114

Couscous Soup

Ideally, you should place the soup in a vessel underneath the couscous so that the grain is steamed over the stock, imparting its flavor. Make sure you buy coarsely ground semolina and not the fine, powdery semolina used by the Italians in pasta.

2 T olive oil
1 C onion, peeled and minced
½ t chile powder
6 C water
1 t salt
1 lb stewing lamb, trimmed and
    cut into bite-size pieces
2 C tomatoes, peeled and cored,
    with juice
3 T tomato paste
2 C potatoes, peeled and diced
1 C prepared chick-peas,
    drained, rinsed, with outer

skins slipped off
1 C fresh sugar pumpkin (or
    buttercup squash), peeled and
    cut into ½-inch pieces
1 C carrots, scraped and diced

Couscous

2 C couscous (roughly ground
    semolina)
¼ t salt
¾ C cold water (approximately)
¼ C sweet butter, melted
¼ C raisins

1. Place the olive oil in a heavy skillet over medium heat, and sauté the onion with the chile powder for about 5 minutes.
2. Place all the remaining ingredients (except the couscous mixture) in a large soup pot. Add the sautéed onion. Clean out the skillet with some of the soup water, and return it to the soup pot.
3. Cover the soup and simmer it over medium-high heat for 1 ½ hours.
4. In a bowl, combine the couscous, salt, and half of the water. Mix it well. Gradually add enough water to work the couscous into a firm ball.
5. Place this ball in the top of a steamer over boiling water. A strainer or colander may be used with a lid or cover of aluminum foil. Steam the couscous approximately 1 hour.
6. Place the steamed couscous in a bowl, and break apart the ball until the grains are separated and no lumps remain. Mix in the butter and raisins. Place 2 heaping tablespoons of couscous in each serving bowl, and ladle plenty of soup broth over each portion.
7. Let the soup set for 5 minutes before eating it. This allows time for the couscous to absorb the broth.

Serves 6

ॐ

CREAM OF ARTICHOKE AND PROSCIUTTO SOUP

For the "hurried gourmet," artichoke hearts come packed in oil or brine. Taste some of the leafy part of the heart to make sure the vegetable isn't tough or stringy. If it is, trim the hearts down to the soft, delectable sections.

2 T clarified sweet butter	16 ozs artichoke hearts pre-
½ lb prosciutto (Italian ham),	served in brine, drained, and
thinly sliced, trimmed of fat,	cut into small pieces
and cut into ½-inch strips	Sprinkle of white pepper
2 T flour	¼ t salt
2 C milk	Freshly grated nutmeg
1 C heavy cream	½ C grated Parmesan cheese

1. Butter is clarified by heating it until the solids separate, leaving the translucent fat on top before pouring off the milky solids. Heat the clarified butter in a large saucepan. Add the prosciutto, and sauté it over medium-low heat for 1–2 minutes.
2. Add the flour, and stir it so that the ham is evenly coated. Slowly add 1 cup of the milk, stirring constantly. Heat the ham 2–3 minutes, then add the other cup of milk.
3. Stirring constantly, heat the soup but do not boil it. Add the heavy cream, artichokes, pepper, salt (taste for salt before adding), and a dash of nutmeg.
4. Before serving, sprinkle Parmesan cheese on each portion.

Serves 4

ॐ

CREAM OF VEGETABLE SOUP

This soup takes approximately 10 minutes to make if you prepare the veal stock ahead of time and save the vegetables. Freeze any remaining stock for later use.

2 C mixed vegetables, cooked	2 T flour
and diced	1 C half-and-half
1½ C veal stock (see *Chlodnik* on	Salt
p. 113)	Freshly grated nutmeg
2 T sweet butter	

1. Pass the vegetables through the fine disc of a food mill over a large bowl. Add the veal stock to the vegetable purée and stir it well.

SOUPS

116

2. Melt the butter in a saucepan over medium-low heat, and whisk in the flour to make a roux.
3. Slowly add the half-and-half while whisking the soup constantly as the béchamel sauce thickens.
4. Add the puréed vegetables and stock to the cream sauce; heat the soup but don't boil it.
5. Add salt to taste (approximately 1 teaspoon if the stock isn't salted). Sprinkle with nutmeg.

Serves 4

ৰু

EGG CONE SOUP

Youngsters will enjoy helping you with this soup. The eggs are fun for lunch boxes and picnics too. Heavy kitchen parchment or foolscap paper may also be used. Egg cones take a bit of practice, so try one or two first.

Water **4 large eggs**
Watercress (1 bunch) **4 C beef stock**
Butter

1. Fill a deep saucepan nearly to the top with water, and bring it to a boil over high heat.
2. Meanwhile, make a 14-inch square of heavy-duty aluminum foil. Fold the square in half with the shiny side inward. Fold this into another square (not a rectangle). Then fold this square on the diagonal into a triangle. Four pockets thus are formed when you separate the folds.
3. Make 4 bouquets of three watercress stems each. Tie the bouquets together with an extra stem, and trim off the stem ends from each bouquet.
4. Place a lump of butter in the point of each aluminum foil pocket.
5. Beat 1 egg in a bowl, and pour it into a pocket. Repeat for each egg until the 4 pockets are filled with a scrambled egg.
6. Gingerly hold the top where the pockets converge, and lower the foil container into the boiling water. Cook the eggs for 7 – 10 minutes until they are quite firm.
7. Place the foil containers in the freezer compartment for 20 minutes.
8. Pour beef stock into a small saucepan, and bring it to a simmer over medium-low heat.
9. To unmold the eggs, carefully unfold the aluminum foil. Trim the egg cones if they have jagged edges.
10. Place an egg cone in each bowl with a watercress bouquet. Ladle hot stock over the cress and egg cones.

Serves 4

MEAT
117

Eggplant Moussaka Soup

Fresh eggplant from your garden sautés much faster than store-bought. The same ingredients as Greek moussaka go into this filling soup, and it's an excellent cornucopia of garden tastes.

3 ½ C water
1 C celery, threaded and diced
1 C carrots, diced
1 ½ C onion, peeled and diced
5 – 7 T olive oil, as needed
1 garlic clove, peeled, crushed, and minced
½ lb ground lamb

1 C potatoes, peeled and diced
4 C eggplant, peeled and cut into ½-inch cubes
½ C tomatoes, peeled, cored, and chopped
¾ T oregano
1 t salt

1. In a large saucepan, bring the water to a boil, add the celery, carrots, and 1 cup of onion, and cook for 10 minutes. Pour the vegetables through a strainer, reserving the liquid and discarding the vegetables. Return the vegetable water to the rinsed pan.
2. In a heavy skillet over a medium-low burner, heat 2 tablespoons olive oil. Add the garlic and the remaining ½ cup of onion, and sauté them a few minutes. Cover and sweat them for 5 – 8 minutes. Remove the onion and garlic with a slotted spoon and reserve.
3. In the same skillet, fry the lamb in the leftover oil for 5 – 7 minutes. Remove the lamb with a slotted spoon and reserve. Discard the oil.
4. Meanwhile, in a separate saucepan over medium heat, boil the potatoes, covered, for 10 minutes.
5. Heat 3 tablespoons of olive oil in a skillet. Add the eggplant and sauté it for 3 – 4 minutes. Stir frequently, and add more oil if it browns too much. Remove the eggplant and reserve.
6. To the stock add the tomatoes, oregano, salt, garlic and onion, lamb, potatoes, and eggplant. Simmer the soup for 10 minutes.

Serves 6

Soups

118

Filet Mignon Soup

The trick to this soup is to have the stock on hand and the vegetables pre-pared before assembling the soup. Then it is only a matter of minutes to put this soup together. First-class ingredients produce an exquisite, ritzy soup.

⅓ C carrots, scraped and finely
    diced
⅓ C shallots, peeled and finely
    diced
4 T sweet butter
⅛ t thyme
¼ t tarragon leaves, minced
2 T dry white vermouth
4 large mushroom caps, de-
    stemmed and peeled

2 T olive oil
3 C beef stock
1 rasher bacon, diced
½ lb filet mignon (about 1 large
    filet), trimmed of fat
1 T truffles, minced
1 T cognac
Salt
Freshly ground black pepper

1. The carrots and shallots are a *mirepoix*, or fine dice. In a small saucepan over medium heat, melt 2 tablespoons of the butter. Add the *mirepoix*, thyme, and tarragon, and sauté in the butter for 1 minute.
2. Add the vermouth, cover, lower the heat, and sweat the vegetables for 10 minutes.
3. Remove the saucepan from the burner but keep it covered.
4. Cut the mushroom caps into crescent slices (cut these in half if they are too large).
5. Over medium heat in a medium-size skillet, melt remaining 2 table-spoons of butter. Add 1 tablespoon olive oil and the mushrooms. Sauté them 1 minute.
6. Cover the mushrooms and sweat them over low heat for 12 minutes. Drain and reserve them.
7. Heat the stock in a saucepan to the simmering point.
8. In a skillet, heat the remaining 1 tablespoon of olive oil and add the bacon. Render the bacon in the oil over high heat. With a slotted spoon, remove the bacon and discard it.
9. Slice the filet mignon into thin bite-size slices no larger than ¾ of an inch in length. Add the filet mignon and truffles to the oil in the skillet. Sauté the filet a few seconds so the outside of the meat is light brown.
10. Add the *mirepoix*, mushrooms, and cognac. Sauté over medium heat a few seconds more.
11. Add the hot stock.
12. Season with salt and pepper to taste.

Serves 4

FRENCH ONION SOUP

When Les Halles, the central market, still operated in Paris, the thing to do was to stay up all night to savor a bowl of the French onion soup. Unfortunately, our sleepless night at Les Halles produced memories of a watery, tepid soup with soggy croutons. In this version the toasted day-old bread rounds stay crisp on top, while the cream adds a rich, velvety smoothness to the onion stock. From the casserole or skillet on the table, ladle the soup into individual gratin bowls, continental style. Follow it by a tossed salad with mustard-oil-vinegar dressing and a cheese and fresh fruit dessert tray.

¼ C sweet butter
2 C onion, peeled and sliced parallel to the top in ¼-inch slices
5 C beef stock (or *Beef Espresso Consommé* on p. 105)

¼ C dry red wine
1 crusty baguette cut into 1-inch-thick slices left standing 1 day
½ C heavy cream
1 C grated Parmesan cheese

1. In an 8- or 10-inch iron or enameled skillet over medium heat, melt the butter.
2. Simmer the onion, covered, in the butter 5–8 minutes.
3. Add the stock. Bring it to a boil. Reduce the heat and boil slowly, covered, for 25 minutes.
4. Add the wine. While the soup simmers another 5 minutes, toast the bread slices on both sides under a broiler. Remove the skillet from the burner, and let the soup sit 2–3 minutes. Stir in the cream.
5. Float the toasted French bread on top of the soup in the skillet, and sprinkle it generously with Parmesan cheese. Reserve a little cheese to serve in a small dish at the table.
6. Place the soup under a broiler until the bread tops sizzle (approximately 2 minutes). Using potholders to protect your hands, place the skillet on the table.

Serves 4

SOUPS

GOULASH SOUP

The Budapest gulyás, the Hungarian national stew, is a thick dish of pork and sauerkraut and sometimes veal. This is an Americanized soup version that retains the characteristic paprika and wine undertaste. This soup also may be made with quality ground beef.

⅛ lb bacon, sliced and diced
1 T olive oil
¾ lb stewing beef, trimmed of fat
    and cut in ½-inch pieces
1 C onion, peeled and diced
2 t Hungarian paprika
¼ t caraway seeds
⅛ t marjoram
1 garlic clove, peeled and minced

6 C beef stock
2 C tomatoes, peeled, with juice
¼ C burgundy wine
Pinch of sugar
1 C broad egg noodles
2 T tomato paste
Salt
Sour cream

1. In a heavy soup pot over medium heat, fry the bacon in olive oil until it's golden brown.
2. Add the beef and onion, and sauté them over medium heat for 5 minutes. With a slotted spoon, drain off excess grease.
3. Add the paprika, caraway seeds, marjoram, and garlic to the beef. Stir briefly.
4. Add the stock, tomatoes, wine, and sugar. Bring the soup to a boil, lower the heat, and simmer, covered, over medium-low heat for 1 hour.
5. Bring the soup to a boil and add the noodles. Simmer at a low boil for 20 minutes until the noodles are firm but cooked. Stir in the tomato paste to thicken. If the beef stock is salted, additional salt won't be required, but taste for salt.
6. Serve with a dollop of sour cream in each bowl.

Serves 6

MEAT
121

꙰

LAMB APRICOT SOUP

This is a zingy soup version of a Moroccan stew called tagine. *It marries salty and sweet flavors in a tantalizing, spicy base.*

4 T olive oil
1 ¼ lb stewing lamb, in bite-size
    pieces
½ C onion, peeled and diced
2 garlic cloves, peeled, crushed,
    and minced
¼ t cayenne
⅛ t ground cloves
¼ t Tabasco sauce

¼ t Hungarian paprika
¼ t sugar
1 C dried apricots, chopped
2 C dry white wine
4 C beef stock
2 t fresh mint leaves, de-
    stemmed and minced
2 C cooked white rice

1. Place the oil in a heavy Dutch oven or soup pot, and sauté the lamb over high heat.
2. Reduce the heat to medium. Add the onion, cover, and sweat for 5–8 minutes, stirring occasionally to prevent browning.
3. Add the garlic, cayenne, cloves, Tabasco sauce, paprika, and sugar. Stir well.
4. Add the apricots, wine, and stock. Bring the soup to a boil.
5. Lower the heat, cover the soup, and simmer for 1 hour.
6. Add the mint before serving. Place the rice in a large serving bowl on the table to be eaten with the soup.

Serves 4

꙰

LAMB SHANK SOUP

We usually recommend cooking vegetables as little as possible to retain vitamins and freshness and to impart taste and texture. But all is not lost because this soup is covered while cooking. The beans are succulent and the lamb tender in true Greek fashion. Orzo is a rice-shaped pasta often used in Greek and Italian dishes.

3 T olive oil
2 lamb shanks
½ C onion, peeled and diced
1 garlic clove, peeled, crushed,
    and minced
¼ C parsley, de-stemmed and
    minced
1 ½ C meatless tomato sauce

¾ C dry white wine or dry white
    vermouth
3 C beef or veal stock
3 C water
1 lb green beans (ends trimmed),
    snapped into 1-inch pieces
⅛ t allspice
2 T orzo

1. Heat the olive oil in a large Dutch oven or soup pot with a lid. Brown the shanks over high heat. Make sure they're dark brown on all sides.
2. Remove the shanks to a plate and reserve. Lower the heat under the pot and add the onion, garlic, parsley, tomato sauce, and wine. Cover and simmer for 5 minutes.
3. Return the lamb shanks to the pot. Add the stock, water, green beans, and allspice. Bring the soup to a boil.
4. Lower the heat to medium-low and simmer the soup, covered, for 1 ½ hours.
5. Add the orzo and simmer another ½ hour.
6. Remove the shanks, and cut the meat from them (if the meat hasn't already fallen into the soup). Discard the bones, and return the meat to the hot soup.

Serves 4 – 6

ॐ

LAMB SOUP

This soup is so thick and chunky that you might be tempted to call it a stew. Soup or stew, it's a cinch to make and a one-pot time-saver.

2 lbs stewing lamb, in 1-inch pieces	**1 t dill, minced**
	½ bay leaf, crushed
1 ½ C potatoes, peeled and quartered	**2 garlic cloves, peeled, crushed, and minced**
3 C tomatoes, peeled and sliced	**3 C beef stock**
1 C onion, peeled and diced	**Salt**
½ t sage, minced	**Freshly ground black pepper**
1 t fennel, minced tops	**2 T flour**

1. Place all the ingredients, except the flour, in a large soup pot, and bring the liquid to a boil.
2. Reduce the heat and simmer, covered, for 1 hour.
3. If necessary, thicken the soup by mixing the flour with ½ cup of tepid stock, and return the mixture to the pot.

Serves 4 – 6

LEEK AND OATMEAL SOUP

This soup has an Irish flair and originally was made with mutton stock. Lamb stock may be substituted if you prefer it to beef. Oatmeal and bran are said to lower cholesterol and provide a healthy addition to soups and stews.

5 C beef stock
2 T oatmeal
2 C leeks (white part only), well washed and finely sliced
⅛ t freshly grated nutmeg

½ t salt
Sprinkle of white pepper
2 T oat bran
3 T cream

1. Boil the stock in a large soup pot over high heat, and add the oatmeal. Boil it for 2 minutes.
2. Add the leeks, lower the heat, cover, and simmer the soup for 40 minutes.
3. Add the nutmeg, salt, and pepper.
4. Slowly sprinkle the oat bran in the boiling soup, stirring with a whisk. Cook at a low boil for 2 minutes, stirring frequently.
5. Before serving add the cream, and heat but don't boil the soup.

Serves 4

LEGUME SOUP

Most stores carry packages of assorted beans, peas, and lentils. Dry legumes are high in protein and each type has a different mineral content. Lentils, for instance, are high in iron, peas in niacin. The variety makes good all-around nutrition.

1 lb confetti beans (a variety package of lentils, peas, and beans)
10 C water
1 smoked ham hock
2 T mild jalapeño chiles, de-seeded and diced

1 garlic clove, peeled, crushed, and minced
½ C onion, peeled and diced
½ C celery, threaded and diced
Salt
Sour cream

1. Wash the beans well. In a heavy soup pot or Dutch oven, add the beans to the water and bring to a boil.
2. Boil the beans for 10 minutes. Cover and remove the beans from the burner. Let them stand, covered, for 1 hour.
3. Add the ham hock, chiles, garlic, onion, and celery. Bring the soup to a boil. Lower the heat and simmer it for 1 hour.

4. The ham hock will be salty so taste the stock before salting.
5. With a slotted spoon remove 1 cup of beans, and place them in a blender with 1 cup of the stock. Purée well.
6. Return the purée to the soup and reheat.
7. Place a dollop of sour cream in each soup serving.

Serves 6 – 8

&

MEAT BORSCHT

When the recipe was given to us, it was emphasized that "this is an approximate recipe in conversational style." So don't worry too much about exact measurements. If you have an extra carrot or beet, put it in. The longer the soup simmers, and the oftener it is warmed up, the better it becomes.

2 lbs chuck beef
Water to cover (approximately 4 C)
1 C beets, peeled, cooked, and diced
6 C cabbage, shredded
1 C carrots, shredded
1 6-oz can tomato paste
⅓ C white vinegar
Bouquet garni (see right)

2 – 4 additional C water
1 t sugar
Salt to taste
Sour cream

BOUQUET GARNI

4 parsley sprigs
6 peppercorns
2 bay leaves

1. Trim the fat or gristle from the beef, and cut the meat into small bite-size pieces.
2. Cover the meat with water in a saucepan.
3. Bring the water to a boil, cover, lower the heat, and boil slowly.
4. After the meat is tender, cooking should take at least 1 ½ hours at a low boil. Strain off the stock and reserve the meat.
5. Place all the vegetables in a large soup pot with the meat stock, tomato paste, and vinegar.
6. Tie the bouquet garni in cheesecloth or place in a tea infuser, and add it to the soup.
7. Simmer the vegetables for 30 minutes. Add the meat, and cook another 30 minutes over low heat, pouring in additional water (2 – 4 cups) if the soup thickens too much.
8. Add the sugar and salt to taste.
9. Remove the bouquet garni, and ladle the borscht into bowls, adding a dollop of sour cream.

Serves 6

MEAT

125

Meatball Soup

Instead of stewing meat for this Middle Eastern dish, cut uncooked lamb off shoulder lamb chops, and process it through a meat grinder. This produces a leaner meatball. Scotch Broth *creates a strong lamb flavor, and you may want to tone down the taste by substituting beef stock.*

½ lb ground lamb
¾ t allspice
1 T parsley, de-stemmed and
   minced
¾ t salt
Freshly ground black pepper
1½ T currants
1½ T pine nuts
1 small egg, slightly beaten
Flour

3 T olive oil
4 C lamb stock (see *Scotch Broth*,
   steps 1 and 2, p. 137)
½ C onion, peeled and diced
1 garlic clove, peeled, crushed,
   and minced
2 t fresh lemon juice
¼ C orzo
Salt

1. Place the lamb in a large mixing bowl. Mix in the allspice, parsley, salt, pepper to taste, currants, and pine nuts.
2. Stir in the egg. Form teaspoon-size balls (about 18), roll them in the flour, and set aside.
3. Heat the oil for frying in a wok or heavy skillet, and brown the meatballs 4 at a time. They need to be browned only on the outside and will cook later in the stock. Remove them with a slotted spoon, and set them aside on an absorbent paper towel.
4. In a large saucepan, bring the stock to a boil. Add the onion, garlic, lemon juice, and meatballs. Simmer for 15 minutes.
5. Add the orzo and salt to taste. Cook another 15 minutes.

Serves 4

SOUPS
126

MIDDLE EASTERN
VEGETABLE SOUP

A highly flavorful soup, this fills your bowl and soul with hill-town flavors. The orzo, a rice-shaped pasta, is available now in supermarkets. Falafel (fried ground chick-pea-based balls) stuffed into pita bread makes a complete taste tour.

3 T olive oil
⅔ C onion, peeled and diced
1 lb stewing lamb, cut into 1-inch
   cubes
2 C tomatoes, peeled, with juice
1 C potatoes, peeled and cut into
   bite-size pieces
½ C prepared chick-peas,
   drained, with skins removed
½ C string beans, cut into bite-
   size pieces

4 C water
2 T parsley, de-stemmed and
   minced
¾ t dried spearmint, crushed
¼ t Hungarian paprika
½ C baby lima beans
¼ C orzo
½ t salt
Freshly ground black pepper

1. Heat the oil in a large heavy soup pot. Add the onion and sauté 5–7 minutes.
2. Add the lamb and sauté it 5 minutes so it browns.
3. Add the tomatoes, potatoes, chick-peas, string beans, and water. Bring the soup to a boil.
4. Stir in the parsley, spearmint, and paprika. Cover and cook for 40 minutes.
5. Add the lima beans and orzo. Cook for 20 minutes more until the orzo is done.
6. Season with salt and pepper to taste.

Serves 4–6

MEAT
127

꧁

Minestrone alla Fiori

Minestrone is always served with a bowl of Parmesan cheese on the table. Whether Nilda Fiori, a spunky northern Italian, was making veal scaloppine, osso buco (veal shanks), or spaghetti Bolognese, her first step was to mix a pesto of garlic, parsley, basil, olive oil, and Parmesan cheese. Minestrone is an Italian vegetable soup, and no two come out alike. So be creative.

1 beef bone
8 C cold water
⅓ C cooked dry white beans
   (canned drained beans may be
   used)
2 C tomatoes, peeled, with juice
3 garlic cloves, peeled and
   crushed
8–10 parsley sprigs, de-stemmed
5–6 fresh basil sprigs, washed
   and de-stemmed

3 T olive oil
2 T grated Parmesan or Romano
   cheese
1 C carrots, scraped and diced
1½ C potatoes, peeled and quartered
2 C spinach or other greens,
   washed, de-stemmed, and
   shredded
Salt
1 C uncooked pasta

1. Place the bone in a large soup pot and add the water.
2. Bring the water to a boil, skimming off scum when necessary.
3. Add the beans and tomatoes. Cover and boil slowly for 30 minutes.
4. Meanwhile, crush the garlic cloves and mince them with the parsley and basil, using a mezza luna or other sharp chopping tool. This mixture forms a *pesto* base.
5. Place the *pesto* in a mortar or small heavy bowl, and blend in the olive oil and grated Parmesan. Let the mixture stand, covered, at room temperature.
6. After the tomatoes and beans have cooked 30 minutes, add the other vegetables to the soup.
7. Boil slowly, covered, for another 30 minutes.
8. Remove pieces of potato with a slotted spoon. Place the potatoes in a shallow bowl, and mash them well into 1 cup of soup stock.
9. Return the mashed potatoes and *pesto* to the soup pot.
10. Salt to taste.
11. Reheat the minestrone to a boil and add the pasta. (Vermicelli broken into small pieces, small bows, thin macaroni, or any other type of pasta may be used.)
12. Boil with the lid slightly ajar for approximately 15 minutes. The pasta should be *al dente*.

Serves 6 – 7

MINTED LAMB LENTIL SOUP

Greek in origin, this soup combines the strong, persuasive flavors of lamb and mint. To heighten the spectrum of colors, use both red and green sweet peppers and orange and green lentils.

5 C water
1 C beef stock
1 ½ C orange or green lentils
1 t salt
¼ C olive oil
1 C onion, peeled and diced
1 garlic clove, peeled, crushed, and minced
¾ C sweet red bell pepper, seeded, cored, and diced
1 C carrots, scraped and diced

2 T dried spearmint (or fresh, if available)
½ t basil
½ t marjoram
⅛ t thyme
Freshly ground black pepper
½ lb lean ground lamb
2 C tomatoes, peeled, with juice
½ C water
2 T fresh lemon juice

1. Pour the water and stock into a large soup pot. Add the lentils and salt, and bring them to a boil. Lower the heat to medium, and continue to cook the lentils at a low boil (15 minutes for orange lentils and 30 minutes for green).
2. In a large skillet over high heat, heat the olive oil.
3. Add the onion, garlic, sweet pepper, carrots, and herbs to the oil. Add a sprinkle of pepper to the simmering vegetables. Cover the skillet, and cook the vegetables over medium heat for 10 minutes.
4. Add the lamb, stirring it into the simmering vegetables. Leave the mixture uncovered, and continue simmering for 5 minutes. (If the lamb is fatty, drain off excess oil.)
5. Add the tomatoes and juice to the lentils along with the sautéed vegetables and the lamb, cleaning out the skillet with ½ cup of water and adding this to the soup pot.
6. Cook the soup, covered, over medium heat for 40 minutes until all the flavors are blended, adding more water if it's too thick. Stir in the lemon juice just before serving.

Serves 6

MEAT

129

Mushroom Soup

In this recipe, the egg yolk and blended mushrooms thicken the soup. Yet delicate morsels of mushrooms are still afloat to titillate the palate. Washed mushrooms don't sauté well because of the added moisture, so peel them. A scoop of freshly whipped cream on each serving is different and highlights the creamy consistency.

3 C mushrooms, peeled and
    sliced
3 T sweet butter
4 t shallots, peeled and minced
⅛ t thyme
1 t parsley, de-stemmed and
    minced
⅛ t rosemary

3 T dry sherry
2 T flour
2½ C beef stock
1 egg yolk
1 C light cream
Dash of nutmeg
Whipped cream (optional)

1. Peel the mushrooms, removing the woody stems, and slice them into crescents. (Approximately 1 pound mushrooms yields 3 cups.)
2. Melt the butter in a saucepan over medium heat, and sauté the mushrooms, shallots, thyme, parsley, and rosemary for 5 minutes until the mushrooms are limp.
3. Add the sherry and cook, covered, 5 more minutes.
4. Remove the pan from the heat. Add the flour and stir well.
5. Slowly add the beef stock, stirring constantly.
6. Return the pan to low heat, and bring the liquid to a low boil.
7. In a separate bowl, beat the egg yolk, cream, and nutmeg together with a whisk.
8. Again remove the pan from the heat. Add the cream mixture, stirring constantly.
9. Place 1 cup of the soup (making sure to include approximately ½ cup mushrooms) in a blender and purée well.
10. Return the blended cup of soup to the pan and reheat (do not boil).

Serves 4

SOUPS

NAVY BEAN SOUP

Navy beans aren't always called "navy" beans on the package. They are a small white bean that New Englanders often use for baked beans. Some beans have been treated so that soaking is unnecessary. If no directions appear on the package, soak or parboil them. It will reduce the cooking time. Using the smoked ham hock, rather than salt pork or pork hock, imparts a more distinctive flavor.

1 C navy beans (soaked overnight or parboiled for 10 minutes and left standing, covered, for 1 hour)
7 C hot water
1 C tomato juice (or vegetable-tomato juice)
1 smoked ham hock
1 bay leaf
¾ C onion, peeled and diced
½ C carrots, scraped and diced

½ C celery, threaded and diced
1 garlic clove, peeled and minced
½ C milk
1 C cooked potatoes, peeled and diced
1 t sweet butter, melted
Salt
Sprinkle of white pepper
2 t white vinegar
1 pinch crushed red pepper

1. Drain and wash the presoaked or parboiled beans. Discard any floating beans or skins.
2. Place the beans in a large soup pot, and cover them with the 7 cups of water and the tomato juice.
3. Over medium-high heat, bring the contents to a boil. Add the ham hock, bay leaf, onion, carrots, celery, and garlic.
4. Reduce the heat. Cover and boil slowly until the beans are tender. (Start sampling after an hour.) The beans must be soft, but not cooked so long that the skins fall off.
5. Remove the bay leaf and ham hock with a slotted spoon.
6. Pour the vegetables through a strainer into a large bowl, reserving the liquid.
7. Place 2 heaping cups of beans and vegetables, plus 2 cups of liquid, in a blender.
8. Purée the vegetables and beans, and return them to the soup with the whole beans and liquid.
9. Place the milk, potatoes, and butter in a blender and purée. Add this mixture to the pot.
10. Salt and pepper to taste. Reheat the soup. Add the vinegar and crushed red pepper at your discretion.

Serves 6

OKRA SOUP

Okra is a vegetable from the South that has found its way north. In Creole cooking this is the gombo that acts as a thickening agent. The okra pods belong to the attractive flowering hibiscus family.

1 smoked ham hock
5 C water
5 C okra, ends trimmed off,
 sliced into rounds
2½ C whole tomatoes, peeled,
 with juice

1 C sweet green bell pepper,
 cored, seeded, and diced
¼ C fine yellow cornmeal
3 T corn oil
¾ t salt

1. In a soup pot, cover the ham hock with the water and bring it to a boil over high heat.
2. Add 4 cups of okra, then the tomatoes and green pepper. Simmer, covered, at a low boil over medium heat for 1 hour.
3. Place the cornmeal in a bowl, and add the remaining cup of okra. With your fingers, mix the okra pieces well into the cornmeal. Place the okra in a strainer, and gently shake off the excess meal.
4. Heat the oil in a skillet over a high heat. Add the cornmeal-covered okra, and fry it until it's dark and crisp.
5. Salt the soup and the fried okra to taste.
6. Place the crispy fried okra in a separate bowl on the table as a garnish.

Serves 4

OXTAIL CONSOMMÉ JULIENNE

Clarification is a magical process that turns cloudy stock into a crystal clear liquid. Serving consommé in glass bowls or cups enhances this shimmering transparent broth.

1 ½ – 2 lb oxtails (cut into 1-inch pieces)
2 small onions, peeled and quartered
2 T corn oil
8 C cold water
Bouquet garni (see right)
1 t salt
2 egg whites and shells
2 t red currant jelly

2 T sherry
½ C carrots, julienne (matchstick thin strips)
½ C celery, julienne

BOUQUET GARNI

½ bay leaf
3 celery tops, with leaves
3 parsley sprigs
6 peppercorns, crushed

1. Over high heat in a heavy soup pot or Dutch oven (and with the kitchen window open or fan on), brown the oxtails and onions in hot oil. Char the oxtail pieces and onions to make a darker consommé.
2. Add the water and boil the oxtail. Tie the bouquet garni into a square of cheesecloth, or place it in a tea infuser, and drop it into the stock.
3. Simmer the soup, covered, for 1 ½ hours.
4. Place a double layer of wet cheesecloth in a large strainer over a bowl. Strain the stock into the bowl, reserving the oxtails for another meal. Discard the bouquet garni. Add the salt.
5. Refrigerate the oxtail stock overnight or until the fat has congealed on top.
6. To clarify: carefully remove all the fat with a slotted spoon; then pour the consommé through another round of a double layer of wet cheesecloth to extract every fat globule. Add the egg whites and crushed shells to the *cold* consommé, and pour it into a clean stainless steel pan. Over medium heat, whisk the consommé to distribute the egg whites and shells while the consommé heats to a boil. Just after the egg white foams to the top, reduce the heat so the consommé remains at a steady simmer, boiling below the surface. Stop whisking, and the egg will bob to the top, carrying the impurities with it. Simmer the consommé for 20 minutes. Carefully ladle the consommé from under the egg froth and into doubled wet cheesecloth placed in a clean strainer over a deep bowl.
7. Add the currant jelly, sherry, and julienne vegetables to the consommé in the bowl, and return it to a clean stainless steel pan, boiling it for another 5 minutes. Again, egg froth might appear on the top, so merely skim this off the surface with a slotted spoon. A sparkling clear consommé will appear.

Serves 4

Paprikesh Beef Soup

*This fiery soup is not to be served to those of delicate constitution.
Hungarian paprika from the czardas country will set you dancing. Because
of the saltiness of the ham and sauerkraut and the punch of the paprika,
taste the soup before adding salt and pepper.*

½ lb stewing beef
¼ C corn oil
1 ½ C onion, peeled and diced
3 C beef stock
2 C water
½ t cumin

1 C sauerkraut, undrained
½ C sour cream
2 C plain yogurt
1 T Hungarian paprika
⅓ lb sliced baked ham

1. Trim off gristle and fat, and cut the stewing beef into small, bite-size pieces.
2. Heat the oil in a large soup pot. Sauté the stewing beef until it browns.
3. Add the onion. Cover and simmer the meat and onion over low heat for 15 minutes, stirring occasionally.
4. Add the beef stock, water, cumin, and sauerkraut to the soup pot.
5. Simmer the soup, covered, for 20 minutes.
6. In a bowl mix the sour cream, yogurt, and paprika into a smooth paste.
7. Add this mixture to the soup.
8. Reheat the soup, but don't boil it.
9. Cut the ham into julienne strips, and add them to the soup.

Serves 6

PHILADELPHIA PEPPER POT

This soup is touted as the soup that saved the nation at Valley Forge. Be as creative as the yield of your larder. That's what the Philadelphia cook in charge of bolstering the morale of the revolutionary troops did. He happened to have on hand lots of tripe, veal knuckles, and pepper. If you aren't a tripe lover, simply substitute 2 more cups of veal stock and omit the tripe.

1 lb tripe, rinsed
Water to cover
5 T olive oil
2 rashers bacon, diced
½ C onion, peeled and diced
¾ C leeks (white part only), well
   washed, sliced
2 t marjoram
1 T parsley, de-stemmed and
   minced

4 C veal stock (See *Chlodnik*, p.
   113)
1 t freshly ground black pepper
1 t chile powder
1 C potatoes, peeled and diced
2 T flour
2 T milk
Salt
2 T parsley, de-stemmed and
   minced

1. The day before you prepare this soup, simmer the rinsed tripe in water to cover for 4 hours. Add water so it is always covered. Then refrigerate the tripe with its stock. You should have at least 2 cups.
2. In a heavy iron skillet, heat the oil and add the bacon. Sauté it a few minutes so the bacon flavor permeates the oil. Then remove the pieces with a slotted spoon. (Reserve for bacon bits on a salad.)
3. Add the onion, leeks, marjoram, and parsley. Sauté a few minutes over medium heat. Cover, lower the heat, and sweat the vegetables for 5 – 8 minutes.
4. In a soup pot on another burner, boil the veal stock with 2 cups of the tripe cooking water.
5. Cut the tripe into small pieces, and add 1 cup of tripe to the stock.
6. Add the sautéed onion and leeks, black pepper, chile powder, and potatoes to the pot. Simmer the soup, covered, for 30 minutes.
7. In a measuring cup, make a paste of the flour and milk. Add to the soup, and simmer 3 – 4 minutes until the soup clears and thickens. Salt to taste.
8. Sprinkle each serving with parsley garnish.

Serves 4

PORTUGUESE KALE SOUP

If linguiça isn't available, substitute chorizo (hot Spanish pork sausage).
Pinto beans, kidney beans, and chick-peas sometimes go into this soup. The
main ingredients, however, are kale, linguiça, and potatoes.

4 T olive oil	½ t salt
1 C onion, peeled and diced	Dash of cayenne
1 lb sliced Portuguese linguiça	1 T sugar
sausage	2 C potatoes, peeled and diced
6 C water	1 lb prepared butter beans,
2 C dry red wine	drained and rinsed
1 lb kale, washed, de-stemmed,	
and shredded	

1. In a heavy pot, heat the olive oil.
2. Add the onion and sauté it 2–3 minutes. Cover and sweat the onion 5–8 minutes.
3. Add the linguiça to the onion and sauté it 2–3 minutes.
4. Add the water, wine, kale, salt, cayenne, and sugar to the pot.
5. Cover the soup, and simmer it over medium heat for 1 hour.
6. Add the potatoes, and continue cooking the soup for 15 minutes.
7. Add the beans, and simmer the soup another 15 minutes. Check to see if more liquid is needed. The consistency should be like a thin stew.

Serves 8

RICE DUMPLING SOUP

These irregularly shaped dumplings will double in size and rise to the top of
the stock when they are ready.

⅔ C freshly cooked white rice	1 large egg
¼ C flour	¼ t salt
1 t grated onion, with juice	¼ t Worcestershire sauce
1 T parsley, de-stemmed and	Freshly ground black pepper
minced	4 C beef stock

1. In a bowl, mash the rice with a wooden spoon.
2. In another bowl, combine the rice, flour, onion and juice, parsley, egg, salt, Worcestershire sauce, and pepper. Mix them well.

3. In a saucepan over high heat, boil the stock. Remove the pan from the burner.
4. By the teaspoonful, drop the rice mixture into the stock. Return the pan to the heat, bringing the stock just to the boiling point. Heat but do not boil for 5 minutes.
5. Ladle a few dumplings into each bowl with some of the stock.

Serves 4

&

SCOTCH BROTH

This is a stalwart soup, a family hand-me-down from the bonny industrial hills of Dunkirk, Scotland.

1 ½ lbs lamb shoulder chops
10 C water
Salt
½ C carrots, scraped and diced

½ C celery, threaded and diced
1 C leeks (white part only), sliced
3 T pearl barley
Freshly ground black pepper

1. Place the lamb in a soup pot with the water.
2. Bring it to a boil, and reduce the heat to medium-low. Cook at a low boil, covered, for 1 hour. Salt to taste.
3. Remove the lamb with a slotted spoon. Pour the stock into a bowl, and skim off excess fat.
4. Rinse the soup pot, and return the lamb and stock to the pot, adding the carrots, celery, and leeks. Bring the soup to a boil, and reduce the heat. Cook at a low boil for 30 minutes.
5. Add the barley and cook another 30 minutes.
6. Pepper to taste.
7. Remove the meat and bones with a slotted spoon. Cool them slightly.
8. Cut the meat from the bones into small pieces. Add the lamb meat to the soup and heat.

Serves 4−6

MEAT

Summer Squash Pork Soup

This soup blends Indonesian flavors in a pleasing medley. Freeze ginger-root to grate as needed. Coconut milk may be made by pouring 2 cups of boiling water over 1 cup of grated unsweetened coconut (found in most natural food stores). Let the coconut steep at least 15 minutes. Then strain out the liquid. Commercial coconut-based drink preparations are too sweet and will spoil the recipe.

2 t soy sauce
2 T lime juice
4 lean center-cut pork chops (not too thick)
7 T safflower oil
½ garlic clove, peeled, crushed, and minced
⅔ C red onion, peeled and diced
¼ t turmeric
¼ t cumin
¼ t coriander
½ t curry powder

¼ t gingerroot, peeled and grated
2½ C summer squash (yellow squash or zucchini), cut in thin rounds (select the smaller tender squash)
3½ C brown veal stock (or half beef-half chicken stock)
1 C coconut milk (see commentary below)
A few drops of Tabasco sauce
¼ C slivered macadamia nuts (or grated unsweetened coconut)

1. In a bowl, mix the soy sauce and lime juice as a marinade.
2. Cut the meat from the chops into ¼-inch strips. With a fork, press the strips into the marinade.
3. Pour 2 tablespoons of safflower oil in a soup pot or Dutch oven over high heat. Add the garlic and onion. Sauté a few seconds, reduce the heat, cover, and sweat 5–8 minutes, stirring occasionally.
4. Add the spices, grated gingerroot, and squash. Stir well.
5. Add the stock and coconut milk. Bring the soup to a boil, cover, and simmer it for 25 minutes, covered.
6. During the last 10 minutes, drain the pork strips, reserving the marinade. Pat the pork strips dry on a paper towel.
7. In a wok, heat remaining 5 tablespoons of safflower oil for frying. Add the pork strips, and stir-fry for 8–10 minutes (or until the strips are golden).
8. With a slotted spoon, remove the pork to a plate.
9. When the soup has simmered 25 minutes, add the Tabasco sauce and reserved marinade. Ladle the hot soup into serving bowls.
10. Distribute pork strips equally among the bowls, and sprinkle macadamia slivers (or coconut) on each serving.

Serves 4

VEGETABLE SHORT RIB SOUP

Vegetable soup is universal. This is a family recipe and changes with the season, the generation, and the mood of the cook. Any vegetable on hand may be added, although it should be fresh. Leftover vegetables tend to get mushy.

5 C water
½ C onion, peeled and diced
1 bay leaf
1 T celery leaves, minced
2 lbs short ribs, cut into 3-inch
   pieces
¼ C barley

¾ C potatoes, peeled and diced
¾ C carrots, scraped and diced
⅓ C celery, threaded and diced
1 C cabbage, shredded
1 C tomatoes, peeled, with juice
Salt
Freshly ground black pepper

1. Bring the water, onion, bay leaf, and celery leaves to a boil in a soup pot or Dutch oven.
2. Add the short ribs. Lower the heat and boil slowly for 1 ½ hours.
3. Remove the ribs and reserve.
4. The meat will leave a fat layer floating on top. Degrease the soup with a large spoon.
5. Add the barley to the soup and cook, covered, at a low boil for 30 minutes.
6. Add the vegetables, salt and pepper to taste, and cover. Boil slowly for 20 minutes.
7. Place the ribs in a shallow baking dish, and brown in a preheated 350° F. oven as the vegetables cook.
8. Serve the short ribs in separate dishes at the table.

Serves 6 – 8

MEAT

139

WILD RICE MUSHROOM SOUP

Wild rice is a grass, not a rice. Neither brown nor white rice substitutes for the crunchy, nutty flavor of wild rice. Cook wild rice separately, and drain well because the cooking water has an acrid taste.

3 T sweet butter
12 ozs mushrooms
⅛ t basil
⅛ t imported oregano
⅛ t thyme
2 T onion, peeled and grated, with juice

½ C wild rice
Cold water to cover
6 C beef stock
2 T lemon juice
Lemon slices
Grated Romano or Parmesan cheese

1. In a soup pot over medium heat, melt the butter.
2. Peel the mushrooms and cut off the woody stems. Slice the mushrooms and sauté them in the butter for 2–3 minutes.
3. Add the basil, oregano, thyme, and onion. Cover the pot, and let the mushrooms sweat over medium-low heat for about 10 minutes until they are limp.
4. Wash the wild rice. Place it in a medium-size saucepan, and cover the rice with 3 inches of cold water. Bring it to a boil. Reduce the heat to low and simmer the rice, covered, for 30 minutes.
5. Add the beef stock to the mushrooms. (You may also use half veal or chicken stock.) Simmer them, covered, for 30 minutes.
6. Drain the cooked rice and add it to the soup.
7. Add the lemon juice. Top each serving with a slice of lemon. Place a bowl of grated Parmesan cheese on the table.

Serves 4

Vegetable and Legume

Baſic Grain Stock *143*
Baſic Seaweed Stock (Daſhi) *143*
Baſic Vegetable Stock *144*

SOUPS

BASIC GRAIN STOCK

Victorian cookbooks usually included 1 or 2 receipts for grain broths, recommending them for invalids because they were easy on the digestive system. But you needn't be an invalid to enjoy this broth. Combine it with vegetable stock and a little salt for a nutritious light lunch. Or double the recipe and freeze it as a foundation for the soups that follow.

5 C water	**2 T long-grain white rice**
2 T pearl barley	**2 T millet**

1. In a stockpot over high heat, bring the water to a boil.
2. Add the barley, rice, and millet. Cover the pot and simmer the stock for 45 minutes.
3. Pour the grains into a strainer, reserving the stock in a bowl. Discard the grains (most of the nutrients will be in the stock).

Yields approximately 5 C

BASIC SEAWEED STOCK (DASHI)

This version of Japanese dashi is ready in less than half an hour. Several types of seaweed are available at natural food markets today, but use the sweeter kombu. Dashi has a slight taste of the sea and may be used in miso and fish soups. Because of the soy sauce and seaweed, salt should be used sparingly in recipes used with this stock.

8 C water	**4 t dry sherry**
2 strips dried kombu seaweed	**2 scallions, finely sliced (only if**
4 T soy sauce	**serving as a broth)**
½ t sesame oil	

1. In a stockpot over medium heat, bring the water to a low boil.
2. Pass the seaweed through cold faucet water, and pat it dry with a cloth or paper towel. Place the seaweed in the boiling water. Cover the pot and simmer the seaweed for 10 minutes.
3. Remove the pot from the heat, keep it covered, and steep the kombu for 10 minutes.
4. Stir in the soy sauce, sesame oil, and sherry.
5. If serving as a soup, ladle it into bowls and sprinkle scallions on each.

Yields 8 C

VEGETABLE AND LEGUME

143

BASIC VEGETABLE STOCK

The milder vegetables are best for a basic vegetable stock. Avoid members of the cabbage and pepper families. Leeks always add a wonderful flavor to soups, and they aren't as strong as onions. Potatoes make a good addition, provided you aren't aiming for a clear stock. Save exotic seasonings and herbs for the individual recipes. The idea of a basic stock is to give body to the soup without extraneous flavors calling attention to themselves.

1 C leeks (white part only), well
    washed, chopped
1 C carrots, scraped and
    chopped
½ C tomatoes, peeled, with juice
1 C celery (including a few
    leaves), chopped
1 C lettuce, chopped
½ t salt

8 C water

BOUQUET GARNI

¼ C parsley, de-stemmed
1 garlic clove, peeled and
    crushed
3 peppercorns, crushed
1 sprig fresh thyme
    (or ⅛ t dried)

1. Combine the first 7 ingredients in a stockpot. Add the bouquet garni tied in cheesecloth or held in a tea infuser.
2. Cover the pot and bring the water to a boil. Reduce the heat to medium. Simmer the stock for 45 minutes.
3. Remove the pot from the burner and allow it to stand, covered, for 15 minutes.
4. Pour the vegetables into a sieve, retaining the stock in a bowl.

Yields 8 C

SOUPS

Adzuki Bean Soup

Adzukis are small dark beans native to China and Japan. This Oriental dish is a basic, healthful, peasant-style soup. Note: 4 cups of dashi (see page 143) may be substituted for the water and kombu.

½ C adzuki beans
1 T olive oil
½ C onion, peeled and diced
1 garlic clove, peeled, crushed,
  and minced
4 C water
2 strips kombu seaweed

½ t salt
Freshly ground black pepper
6 drops hot Chinese chile sauce
  (other hot sauces may be substituted)
3 T millet

1. Soak the beans overnight, or cover them with water in a large soup pot. Over high heat bring them to a boil, cover, and let them boil for 10 minutes. Remove the pot from the burner. Do not remove the lid. Let the beans steam, covered, for 2 hours.
2. Drain the beans.
3. In a large heavy soup pot over a medium burner, heat the oil. Add the onion and garlic and sauté them 3–4 minutes.
4. Add the water and kombu and bring them to a boil. Lower the heat and let them simmer for 1 hour, covered, until the beans soften.
5. In a blender, blend the ingredients 2–3 minutes until smooth.
6. Return the bean soup to the pot and add the salt, pepper to taste, chile sauce, and millet. Bring the soup to a boil, lower the heat, and simmer for 15 minutes until the millet softens.

Serves 4

Asparagus Cheddar Cheese Soup

Asparagus always has been considered a delicacy, and cheese makes a natural companion. The problem with most asparagus soups is that they often are too strong. The wine and cheese tone down this soup. Adding only tender asparagus tips avoids the stringiness of whole spears.

24 asparagus spears
½ C water
½ C dry white wine
2 T sweet butter
1 T flour
1 C milk

1 ½ C mild cheddar cheese,
  grated
1 C light cream
¼ t salt
Sprinkle of white pepper

1. To prepare fresh asparagus, cut off the stalk base, leaving approximately 5 inches of the spears.
2. In a saucepan over high heat, bring the water and wine to a boil and drop in the spears. Cover and simmer them for 7 – 10 minutes, until they're tender. Pour them through a strainer, reserving the cooking water and the spears in separate bowls.
3. Rinse the saucepan, and over medium-low heat melt the butter to make a roux with the flour. Stir constantly with a whisk as you slowly add the milk. Don't boil this white sauce.
4. Add the cheddar cheese, and stir it into the sauce until it's melted. Remove the pan from the burner.
5. On a cutting board, place the spears in the same direction in a row, and cut off the tips (approximately 1 inch). Reserve.
6. Using the finest disc, work the remaining stalks through a food mill into a bowl with the asparagus cooking water. (A food mill strains out the fibers whereas a blender only cuts them finer.)
7. Add this asparagus purée to the cheese mixture.
8. Cut the asparagus tips into ½-inch pieces, and add them to the soup. Add the cream, stir well, and reheat but do not boil the soup.
9. Salt and pepper to taste.

Serves 4 small portions

℀

Asparagus Hollandaise Soup

This is a wonderful soup to welcome in the spring. Although it has a hollandaise-style base, it isn't as rich as a sauce. Yet it retains the hint of lemon and eggs. A dash of turmeric lends the soup a daffodil color to contrast with the fresh green asparagus spears.

1 lb asparagus stalks (about 2 C trimmed)	2 T lemon juice
3 C water	3 C milk
3 T sweet butter	2 T flour
2 egg yolks (extra large)	¼ t salt
3 T prepared mayonnaise	Sprinkle of white pepper
	⅛ t turmeric

1. To prepare the asparagus, start at the flower head of the stalk, cutting into 1-inch pieces toward the base. When a sharp kitchen knife will not cut effortlessly through the stalk, stop and discard the remainder. (This may be half the stalk if the asparagus is not freshly picked.)

2. In a large pot, bring the water to a boil and add the asparagus spears. Cover and boil them for 8 minutes or until tender, then drain them well, reserving the stalks.
3. Meanwhile, in a large saucepan over low heat, melt the butter. Remove the pan from the heat. While stirring with a whisk, add the yolks, mayonnaise, and lemon juice.
4. In a cup, mix ½ cup of milk with the flour, and mix it into a paste.
5. Over a medium-low burner, heat the egg hollandaise, whisking as the yolks cook for 2–3 minutes. Slowly add the remaining 2½ cups of milk, whisking constantly.
6. Add the milk-flour paste and keep whisking the soup.
7. Add the salt, pepper, and turmeric.
8. The soup should be just below boiling. Add the asparagus spears, and bring the soup to just below boiling.

Serves 4

&

BAKED BEAN SOUP

If you don't make your own baked beans, settle for your favorite commercial variety, and this soup will proceed quickly.

¼ C onion, peeled and diced
2 T olive oil
1 ½ C water
1 C tomatoes, peeled, cored, and chopped, with juice
1 ½ C baked beans

¼ t salt
Freshly ground black pepper
2 T red chile sauce, tomato relish, or piccalilli
Sliced dill pickles

1. In a heavy saucepan over medium heat, sauté the onion in the oil. Cover and let them sweat 5–8 minutes.
2. Add the water, tomatoes, and beans. Cover and simmer them 20 minutes.
3. Place the bean mixture in a blender and purée it for 2 minutes.
4. Return the soup to the rinsed saucepan, and bring it to a low boil.
5. Add the salt, pepper, and chile sauce. Serve with pickles.

Serves 4

BREAD MINT SOUP

This minty soup is a good candidate for using up leftover stale bread.
Simply tear the bread into pieces and process it in the blender. Leftover
bread crumbs freeze well in a freezer container.

2 T olive oil
1 small garlic clove, peeled,
  crushed, and minced
½ C onion, peeled and diced
2 ripe tomatoes, peeled, cored,
  and diced

1 C bread crumbs
3 C water
½ t salt
25 – 30 fresh mint leaves,
  coarsely chopped

1. In a soup pot over a medium burner, heat the oil. Sauté the garlic and
   onion 2 – 3 minutes. Cover the pot and let them sweat 5 – 8 minutes,
   stirring occasionally so they don't brown.
2. Add the tomatoes and simmer them, covered, for 15 minutes.
3. Stir in the bread crumbs, blending thoroughly.
4. Add the water, salt, and mint leaves. Cover the soup, and let it simmer
   another 30 minutes.

Serves 4

BROCCOLI RÉMOULADE SOUP

A rich soup, this works especially well in small servings as an appetizer to
roast beef and other meat entrées.

4 C broccoli flowers
2 C water
⅓ C mayonnaise
½ t Dijon-style mustard
1 T dill pickle, minced
1 t capers, drained and diced

2 t parsley, de-stemmed and
  minced
1 t fresh chives, minced
¼ t fresh tarragon, minced
1 C milk
¼ t salt

1. Place the broccoli over the water in a steamer over high heat, and steam
   it for 10 minutes.
2. In a small bowl, mix the mayonnaise, mustard, pickle, capers, parsley,
   chives, and tarragon to form a rémoulade.
3. Pour the milk into a blender container. Add the steamed broccoli and
   the rémoulade. Blend for 2 minutes.
4. Pour the soup into a saucepan. Add the salt and heat but do not boil.

Serves 4

⊷

Caraway Milk Soup

Caraway seeds exude a pleasing aromatic oil and often are used in cheeses and breads. The plants originally grew in northern Europe but now are widely cultivated for the tiny, tasty seeds.

3 T sweet butter
1 t caraway seeds
2 T flour
3 C boiling water
1 C thin egg noodles (or broken
  vermicelli)

1 C milk
2 T sour cream
½ t salt
Sprinkle of white pepper

1. In a large skillet over medium-low heat, melt the butter and add the seeds. Cook the seeds 1 minute.
2. Add the flour, whisking for 1 minute. Do not let the butter brown.
3. Add the boiling water ½ cup at a time, whisking well.
4. Reduce the heat and simmer the soup for 15 minutes.
5. Meanwhile, cook the noodles separately as directed and drain them. Reserve.
6. Pour the soup through a strainer into a bowl and discard the seeds. Return the soup to the pot.
7. Add the milk and sour cream. Whisk the soup and heat it but don't boil it.
8. Season with salt and pepper to taste and add the cooked noodles.

Serves 4

⊷

Carrot Leek Soup

Leeks and carrots make a natural complementary couple. Add a little heavy cream and the French call it potage crecy. *This soup is bright orange and high in vitamin A. Not only that, it's delicious.*

4 C water
1 C celery (including the leaves),
  threaded and diced
2 C carrots, scraped and diced
3 fresh tarragon leaves, minced

⅔ C leeks (white part only),
  diced
3 T sweet butter
½ t salt

1. In a soup pot over high heat, bring the water to a boil, and simmer the celery for 10 minutes. Pour it into a strainer and reserve the cooking liquid. Discard the celery.

2. Return the celery water to the pot.
3. Add the carrots and tarragon, and simmer them gently for 10 minutes, until they are tender.
4. Meanwhile, in a frying pan over medium heat, sauté the leeks in the melted butter for 3–4 minutes.
5. Add the sautéed leeks to the carrots in the soup pot, and simmer another 10 minutes.
6. Cool the soup. Place ⅔ of the soup in a blender, and purée it for 2 minutes.
7. Return the purée to the rest of the soup in the pot, reheat, and add the salt.

Serves 4–6

&

CREAM CHEESE SOUP (CHILLED)

Rich and creamy, a little of this simple-to-make soup goes a long way. A quick way to soften the cream cheese: immerse it, foil unwrapped, in hot water for a few minutes.

2 C vegetable stock
8 ozs cream cheese, softened
½ C sour cream
¼ t salt

1 T walnut oil
2 t fresh lemon juice
2 t walnuts, finely ground

1. Heat the stock to a simmer in a large saucepan over medium heat.
2. In a small bowl, use a wooden spoon to blend the cream cheese and sour cream into a smooth mixture.
3. Add the cream cheese mixture to the hot stock, and blend it with a whisk.
4. Stir in the salt, oil, and lemon juice. Chill.
5. Place in small serving bowls, and garnish with the ground walnuts.

Serves 4

SOUPS

150

CREAM OF BRUSSELS SPROUT SOUP

Many shy away from members of the cabbage family because they cause digestive problems. A slice of bread attracts the strong odors and gaseous molecules. In cooking the sprouts separately, you lose some vitamins, but the sprouts still retain their fiber content. This soup has a surprisingly delicate flavor.

1 lb brussels sprouts	2 ½ C milk
Water	1 C light cream
Slice of stale white bread	½ t salt
3 T sweet butter	Sprinkle of white pepper
3 T flour	Freshly grated nutmeg

1. Trim the sprouts. If they're young and fresh (no larger than a thimble), they'll need little trimming. If not, remove the tough base where the sprout attaches to the stalk and some of the outer leaves.
2. In a large pot, cover the sprouts with water, and over high heat bring them to a boil. Add the bread (a leftover heel of bread works well), and cover the pot immediately. Make sure to use the kitchen fan. Remove the bread with a slotted spoon after the sprouts have boiled 6 – 7 minutes.
3. Simmer the sprouts until they're tender and a fork or knife pierces them easily. This depends on the size and freshness of the sprouts — from 10 – 25 minutes.
4. Over medium heat in a soup pot, melt the butter.
5. Add the flour, and whisk it into a roux for a few seconds. Add 1 ½ cups of milk. Whisk the soup 2 – 3 minutes until it thickens, then add the other cup of milk and whisk it for 2 – 3 minutes until the soup again thickens.
6. Drain the sprouts, and place them in a blender with the cream. Blend a second — no longer. Stir the mixture, and blend it a second more. (You don't want a purée.)
7. Return the sprout mixture to the soup pot, and stir it into the soup.
8. Reheat thoroughly without boiling, adding the seasonings.

Serves 4

VEGETABLE AND LEGUME

CREAM OF CELERY SOUP

This is a popular soup that may be used as a basis for casserole dishes. It is easy to prepare and a standard which is handy to have in your soup repertoire.

1 C celery, threaded and diced	3 T flour
¼ C onion, peeled and diced	½ t salt
2 C water	Sprinkle of white pepper
2 C milk	

1. In a covered soup pot over medium-high heat, cook the celery and onion in the water for 30 minutes.
2. Add 1 ½ cups of milk. Reduce the heat to a simmer.
3. In a separate bowl, mix the flour with the remaining ½ cup of milk to a smooth paste.
4. Whisk the paste into the soup, and turn up the heat to bring the soup nearly to a boil. Simmer 15 minutes, stirring frequently, until the soup thickens.
5. Add salt and pepper to taste.

Serves 4–6

CREAM OF MUSHROOM SOUP

Why buy a can when this is so easy, fresh, and good? Cream of mushroom forms a foundation for casserole dishes but also stands on its own as an all-time favorite. This recipe requires about 12 ounces of whole mushrooms.

3 T sweet butter	3 T flour
2 C mushroom caps, peeled and diced	½ t salt
1 t onion, grated with juice	Sprinkle of white pepper
3½ C milk	Freshly grated nutmeg

1. In a heavy soup pot over medium heat, melt the butter.
2. Add the mushrooms and onion. Sauté over medium-low heat for approximately 3 minutes.
3. Cover and let the mushrooms sweat for 10 minutes.
4. Add 3 cups of milk and heat it to scalding.
5. Place the flour in a small bowl. Add remaining ½ cup of milk, and stir it with a whisk to make a smooth paste.

6. Add the paste to the soup pot, and continue to simmer the soup for 10 minutes, stirring frequently with a whisk as the soup thickens.
7. Add the salt, white pepper, and nutmeg.

Serves 4

&

CREAM OF TOMATO SOUP

Cream of Tomato Soup *plays a variety of roles. Try a few cups of this recipe on your favorite cooked pasta. Or serve it as a contrast in taste and color along with a slice of spinach quiche.*

2 T sweet butter
3 T flour
2 C milk
½ C heavy cream
1 ½ C fresh tomatoes, peeled,

cooked, seeded, and puréed
(or 1 ½ C prepared tomato
sauce)
2 T tomato paste
½ t salt

1. In a soup pot over medium heat, melt the butter.
2. Make a roux, whisking the flour into the butter.
3. Add 1 cup of milk and simmer, whisking 2–3 minutes until the mixture thickens. Add the remaining cup of milk. Again, whisk until it thickens (just to scalding). Never boil the soup.
4. Add the cream. Whisk in the puréed tomatoes and paste.
5. Heat to scalding.
6. Add the salt.

Serves 4

&

CURRY SOUP

Kohlrabi out of season may be tough and need trimming, especially at the root end. The knife should pierce the bulb without force. Curry is a blend of spices, and some prefer to prepare it in the home. Make sure the curry is fresh. Chutney is found in the specialty section of most supermarkets. Serve this Indian soup with Indian flat breads — poppadums or chapatis.

1 C onion, peeled and diced
4 T safflower oil
¼ t sesame oil
1 ½ C kohlrabi, peeled and diced
  (approximately 4 lbs)
2 t curry powder

6 C vegetable stock
1 C orange lentils, washed and
  drained
1 t salt
Freshly ground black pepper
2 T mango chutney

VEGETABLE AND LEGUME
153

1. Over medium-high heat in a large heavy soup pot, sauté the onion in the oils 2–3 minutes.
2. Add the kohlrabi and stir.
3. Cover the vegetables and let them sweat 5–8 minutes.
4. Add the curry and stir it in well.
5. Add the vegetable stock and lentils, and bring them to a boil over high heat.
6. Reduce the heat and simmer the soup, covered, for 45 minutes.
7. Taste and season with salt and pepper.
8. Add the chutney last.

Serves 4

&

CURRY SOUP (CHILLED)

Curry powder (or paste) may have a dozen or more ingredients, including turmeric, cayenne, ginger, cloves, coriander, and other spices. This dessert soup is relatively mild for a curry-based soup. However, the cream topping subdues any overtones of spiciness.

2 T sweet butter
½ C onion, peeled and diced
1 t curry powder
2 T flour
4 C vegetable stock
Thin 2-inch-long strip of lemon peel
¼ t rosemary
½ C boiling water

3 T almonds, blanched and ground
3 T shredded coconut

TOPPING

1 t dry sherry
1 T apricot preserves
½ C heavy cream

1. In a large saucepan over medium heat, melt the butter. Add the onion, cover, and let the onion sweat for 5–8 minutes.
2. Blend the curry powder and flour into the onion to make a roux. Stir in the stock. Add the lemon peel and rosemary. Cover and simmer for 20 minutes. Cool.
3. Meanwhile, in a small bowl, pour the boiling water over the almonds and coconut. Cover with foil or a plate, and let them steep for 20 minutes.
4. Pour the curry mixture through a strainer into a bowl, and return the contents of the bowl to the rinsed saucepan. Strain the almond-coconut mixture, pressing on the coconut with a wooden spoon to extract the milk in a bowl. Discard the coconut meat.

5. Pour this milk into the curry soup, and bring the soup to a simmer. Cool. Mix the sherry into the apricot preserves. In a bowl, whip the cream until it mounds. Fold in as much of the sherry-preserve mixture as possible without diluting the cream. Spoon the topping onto individual servings.

Serves 6

୬୦

EGG BOUILLABAISSE TOULONAISE

Wide, shallow soup plates are best for bouillabaisse. The saffron tints the potatoes a pale crocus yellow, and the stock also is permeated by this rich color. Bouillabaisse, which literally means to boil gently, has become associated with this saffron-tomato broth of southern France. An exquisite blend of flavors like this assures satisfied guests and high praise for the cook.

3 T olive oil
2 leeks (white part only), thinly sliced
⅓ C onion, peeled and diced
2 ripe tomatoes, cored and quartered
4 medium-size potatoes, peeled and quartered
4 C water
¼ t saffron threads
2-inch strip of orange peel
Bouquet garni (see right)
4 eggs

Water
4 hard French rolls or French bread slices
Mayonnaise

BOUQUET GARNI

⅛ t rosemary
⅛ t thyme
Pinch of fennel seeds
Celery leaves
2 sprigs of parsley
6 peppercorns
Small garlic clove, crushed

1. Heat the oil in a large heavy saucepan over medium heat. Add the leeks and onion, cover, and let them sweat for 5–8 minutes.
2. Add the tomatoes, potatoes, water, saffron, orange peel, and bouquet garni tied in cheesecloth or in a tea infuser. Cover and cook at a low boil approximately 12–15 minutes. Test the potatoes with a fork.
3. Remove the bouquet garni.
4. With a slotted spoon, remove the potatoes and reserve them in a separate bowl. Cover the bowl with foil or a plate to retain the heat.
5. Pour the soup into a strainer over a bowl. Discard the vegetables, but retain the cooking water.
6. Pour this vegetable stock back into the rinsed saucepan and reheat it.
7. In a separate saucepan, poach the eggs over the water.

8. Slice the French rolls in half. If using French bread, cut 2 slices for each serving. Place the bread in flat soup plates.
9. Position a poached egg on the bread. Pour a small amount of the stock over the egg and bread.
10. Serve the potatoes separately topped with a spoonful of mayonnaise.

Serves 4

&

EGGPLANT SOUP (CHILLED)

This is a Middle Eastern appetizer that may be prepared quickly on a hot summer day. Or serve it with sesame crackers or lavash (crisp, flat sesame bread) as a light luncheon. This is also a terrific starter course for a roast leg of lamb.

4 C eggplant, peeled and diced
½ C sweet green or red bell pepper, cored, seeded, and diced
2 garlic cloves, peeled, crushed, and minced

1 t grated onion and juice
½ C olive oil
¼ t salt
Freshly ground black pepper
2 C plain yogurt
4 fresh mint leaves, minced

1. In a heavy skillet over medium heat, sauté the eggplant, sweet pepper, garlic, and onion in the oil. Add salt and pepper. Cover and let the vegetables sweat 8–10 minutes, stirring occasionally to prevent browning.
2. Pour off any excess oil. Place the eggplant mixture in a blender, and blend well for 1 minute.
3. In a bowl, mix the eggplant mixture with the yogurt.
4. Refrigerate at least 2 hours.
5. Sprinkle each portion with mint leaves.

Serves 4

SOUPS

Four Grain Soup

More grains may be added to this soup, but remember that the grains triple and sometimes quadruple in volume when they cook.

2 T olive oil
¼ C potatoes, peeled and diced
¼ C carrots, scraped and diced
¼ C celery, threaded and diced
1 T parsley, de-stemmed and minced
4 C vegetable stock

2 T rolled oats
2 T millet
2 T barley
2 T rice
¼ C tomato sauce
¾ t salt
Freshly ground black pepper

1. Heat the oil in a heavy pot over medium heat and sauté the potatoes, carrots, celery, and parsley for 2 minutes.
2. Add the vegetable stock, and bring it to a boil over high heat. Add the oats, millet, barley, rice, and tomato sauce. Reduce the heat, and simmer the soup for 40 minutes.
3. Add the salt and pepper.

Serves 4

Garbure

The accompanying toasted bread croutons make this soup the typical French country concoction that it is — elegance from leftovers. In preparing the soup, the extra time taken to slice the vegetables thinly reduces cooking time.

¼ C sweet butter
2 leeks (white part only), thinly sliced
1 C turnip, peeled and thinly sliced
1 C celery, threaded and thinly sliced
1 C potatoes, peeled and thinly sliced
1 C onion, peeled and diced

1 C carrots, thinly sliced
2 C green cabbage, finely shredded
1 C cooked white beans, drained
5 C water (or to cover the vegetables)
2 hard French-style rolls
1 oz grated Gruyère cheese
1½ t salt
Sprinkle of white pepper

1. In a large Dutch oven or heavy saucepan over medium-low heat, melt the butter.
2. Add the leeks, turnips, celery, potatoes, onion, carrots, and cabbage. Cover and cook them 15 minutes, stirring occasionally to prevent browning.
3. Add the beans and water. Cover and simmer for another 15 minutes.
4. With a slotted spoon, remove 1 cup of the vegetables, and purée them for 1 minute in a blender. Pour the purée into a small saucepan over medium heat, and cook it until it's reduced and thickened (about 5 minutes).
5. Slice the hard rolls in half. Butter the halves, and fry them face down in a heavy skillet until they're toasted. Spread the thickened vegetable purée on the toasted bread, top them with the grated cheese, and place them on a baking sheet under a broiler for 3–4 minutes.
6. Meanwhile, pour the remaining soup in a blender and purée for 1 ½ minutes. Return the purée to the rinsed soup pot. Add the salt and pepper and reheat.

Serves 4

&

GAZPACHO (CHILLED)

Gazpacho takes only a few minutes to prepare and tastes as fresh as your garden on those do-nothing summer days.

2 C ripe tomatoes, cored and chopped
1 C sweet green bell pepper, cored, seeded, and diced
1 C cucumber, peeled, seeded, and diced
1 garlic clove, minced
2 T Bermuda onion, peeled and chopped

2 T olive oil
3 T fresh lemon juice
1 ½ C tomato-vegetable juice
⅛ t cayenne
½ t salt
2 T bread crumbs
2 T minced herbs of your choice
Water

1. Prepare the tomatoes, green pepper, cucumber, garlic, and onion.
2. Mix the vegetables together. Place half of them in a blender or food processor, and turn it on a few seconds (not too long).
3. Repeat with the remaining vegetables.
4. Place the vegetables in a large bowl. Stir in the olive oil, lemon juice, tomato-vegetable juice, cayenne, and salt.
5. Stir in the bread crumbs.

6. Refrigerate the soup 2 hours or more. It will chill quicker if the ingredients are cold before preparation.
7. Place an herb ice cube in each bowl. To make herb ice cubes, sprinkle herbs on water in ice cube tray and freeze.

Serves 4

&

HERBED VEGETABLE SOUP (CHILLED)

Try this soup at the heart of the garden season. It will gladden guests with fresh offerings and the cook with the fast preparation time.

3 scallions, first 4 inches from trimmed root end, sliced
3 radishes, sliced
2 C cucumber, peeled, seeded, and diced
2 ripe tomatoes, peeled and quartered
½ garlic clove, peeled, crushed, and minced

2 T parsley, de-stemmed and minced
1 T fresh dill, de-stemmed
½ t fresh basil leaves
2 T olive oil
¼ t salt
1 C plain yogurt
½ C half-and-half
2 T sour cream

1. In a large bowl, mix all the vegetables, herbs, oil, and salt.
2. Place half of the vegetable mixture in a blender with the yogurt, and blend 1 minute. Pour this into another bowl or storage dish with a lid.
3. Blend the remaining vegetable mixture with the half-and-half and sour cream for 1 minute. Combine with the first batch.
4. Refrigerate 30 minutes or more.

Serves 4

&

JELLIED TOMATO SOUP (CHILLED)

An aspic is a savory jelly using meat stock. This tomato-based jelly provides cool and colorful relief from midsummer heat waves.

2 envelopes unflavored gelatin
½ C cold vegetable stock
1 C boiling hot vegetable stock
1 t Worcestershire sauce
⅛ t Tabasco sauce

¼ t salt
1 T fresh lemon juice
1 T dry sherry
3 C fresh tomato juice
Lemon slices

1. In a bowl, sprinkle the gelatin into the cold vegetable stock. Add the boiling vegetable stock, and stir until the gelatin is dissolved.
2. Add the Worcestershire sauce, Tabasco sauce, salt, lemon juice, sherry, and tomato juice.
3. Pour the mixture into an 8 x 8-inch glass dish, and refrigerate the soup for at least 2 hours or until jelled but not firm.
4. Spoon the jelled soup into glass cups or bowls. Garnish each portion with a thin lemon slice.

Serves 6

&

KASHA MACKEREL SOUP

Be sure to watch for the bones when eating this soup. This is a filling, substantial soup. Dark oily fish like mackerel work at reducing cholesterol levels in the body. Sardines or herring also may be substituted.

1 lb fresh mackerel, head and
    tail removed, cleaned, split
    full-length down the center
2 T olive oil
6 C vegetable stock
2 T sweet butter

⅓ C kasha (coarsely ground
    buckwheat groats)
1 T lemon juice
½ t salt
Freshly ground black pepper
Small bowl of sour cream

1. In a heavy iron skillet over medium heat, fry the mackerel on both sides in the oil for 8–10 minutes. Place it on a plate, and remove the bones down the center and sides. Remove the skin. Cut the mackerel into soup-spoon-size pieces.
2. In a large saucepan over high heat, bring the stock to a boil. Add the butter and kasha. Cook the kasha about 12–15 minutes. It should be soft.
3. Add the lemon juice, salt, and pepper. Reduce the heat to a simmer.
4. Place the mackerel in the soup. Do not boil or break up the fish by stirring. Heat to just below boiling.
5. Place the sour cream on the table as a topping.

Serves 4–6

MILLET VEGETABLE SOUP

Millet is an easily digested grain and highly nutritious. Use either fresh shitake mushrooms or dried rehydrated ones. If you prefer, chicken or beef stock may be substituted for the vegetable stock. This soup must be eaten right away. If it stands, the grain will soak up the stock, turning it into a porridge.

¼ C olive oil
½ C onion, peeled and diced
½ C celery, threaded and diced
1 garlic clove, peeled, crushed, and minced
¼ C shitake mushrooms, de-stemmed and sliced
½ C carrots, scraped and diced
2 T parsley, de-stemmed and minced

1 T celery leaves, minced
2 t fresh dill (or dried), de-stemmed and minced
⅛ t thyme
¼ t imported oregano
5 C vegetable stock
½ C millet
1 t salt

1. Heat the oil in a large soup pot over high heat. Add all of the next 10 ingredients. Sauté for 5 minutes.
2. Cover the pot, reduce the heat to a simmer, and sweat the vegetables for 5–8 minutes.
3. Add the stock and bring the soup to a boil. Add the millet.
4. Cover, reduce the heat, and simmer the soup for 35 minutes.
5. Add the salt and serve immediately.

Serves 4–6

ONION AND CHEESE SOUP

A cream-style onion soup, this may be prepared in short order. Two large onions provide enough rings for this naturally sweet soup. Substitute cheddar cheese for a slightly stronger soup.

3 T sweet butter
2 T olive oil
3 C onion (cut and separated into rings)
1 C celery, threaded and diced
3 T flour
2 ½ C milk

1 C vegetable stock
2 slices of white bread
1 C grated Monterey Jack cheese
½ t salt
Sprinkle of white pepper
Freshly ground nutmeg

1. In a large saucepan over medium heat, melt the butter with the oil. Add the onion and celery. Cover, reduce to low heat, and sweat them 5–8 minutes, stirring occasionally.
2. Place the flour in a small mixing bowl. Pour in ½ cup of milk, and using a whisk blend it into a smooth paste.
3. Pour the vegetable stock and the remaining milk into the onion mixture, and bring them to a light boil.
4. Stir in the milk-flour mixture. Simmer for 5 minutes until the soup thickens.
5. Meanwhile, place the bread slices on a baking sheet or foil under a broiler to toast them. Turn the slices over. Sprinkle ⅓ cup of cheese on the untoasted side, and return them to the broiler until the cheese melts. Cut the bread into 1-inch crouton squares.
6. Add the salt, pepper, and nutmeg to the soup. Stir the remaining ⅔ cup of cheese into the soup, and simmer it 2–3 minutes until the cheese melts.
7. Ladle the soup into serving bowls, and garnish with the cheese croutons.

Serves 4

&

ORANGE LENTIL SOUP

This is a bright orange soup. Sometimes orange lentils are referred to as red. They cook faster than the green lentils, and the skins aren't as tough.

½ C orange lentils	2 T sweet butter
1 C carrots, scraped and diced	2 T olive oil
3½ C water	½ t fresh tarragon leaves,
¾ C onion, peeled and diced	minced
1 garlic clove, peeled and minced	1 t salt

1. In a large soup pot over medium-high heat, simmer the lentils and carrots in the water, covered, for 20 minutes.
2. In a skillet over medium-high heat, sauté the onion and garlic in the butter and olive oil for 2–3 minutes. Cover and let them sweat 5–8 minutes, stirring occasionally.
3. Add the onion mixture to the carrots and lentils. Remove the soup pot from the burner, and let the contents cool.
4. Pour the lentil-carrot mixture into a blender container, adding the tarragon leaves and salt.
5. Blend for 2 minutes so the soup is puréed. Return the purée to the soup pot and reheat.

Serves 4

BLACK BEAN SOUP

WASH BEANS, SOAK OVERNIGHT IN 8 CUPS OF WATER. IN 2 TBLS. OF OIL, BUTTER OR MARGARINE SAUTE THE FOLLOWIN UNTIL SOFT AND OPAQUE BUT NOT BROWN, 2 MEDIUM ONION CHOPPED, 1 CLOVE OF MINCED GARLIC, 2 MEDIUM CARROTS CHOPPED, AND 1 STALK OF CHOPPED CELERY. DRAIN THE BEANS AND ADD TO VEGETABLES. TIE BOUQUET GARNI IN A PIECE OF DAMP CHEESECLOTH ADD THIS AND A 1 LB. PIECE OF HAM OR CANADIAN BACON, 1 OZ. BEEF STOCK. BRING TO A SIMMER-SKIMMING OFTEN. PLACE COVER OVER 2/3 OF POT COOK OVER LOW HEAT 2 HOURS. WHEN BEANS ARE TENDER DISCARD GARNI. PUREE HALF AND MIX BACK TOGERTHER. AT THIS TIME YOU MAY ADD 1/8 CUP OF SHERRY IF DESIRED. EITHER DISCARD HAM OR CUT IT INTO SMALL PIECES AND RETURN TO SOUP. SERVE WITH A GARNISH OF LEMON SLICES. GOES WELL WITH STEAMED OR BOILED LOBSTER.

Pea Pod Lettuce Soup

This soup is fresh and sweet. Today most of the shelling peas have edible pea pods as well. Many recipes for this popular soup call for sugar, which seems anathema because fresh peas are sweet naturally. Freeze the remaining vegetable water for other soups.

1 lb shelling peas
3 C water
2 C Boston lettuce (one small head), chiffonade
2 scallions (6 inches from root end), trimmed and sliced
Bouquet garni (see right)
1 T sweet butter

2 T flour
½ C heavy cream
½ t salt

BOUQUET GARNI

4 – 5 fresh mint leaves
2 – 3 sprigs of parsley
Pinch of thyme

1. Shell the peas, reserving the pods. One pound should yield approximately 1 cup of shelled peas.
2. Wash the pods and chop half of them (3 cups).
3. In a large pot over high heat, bring the water to a boil. Add the shelled peas, the 3 cups of chopped pods, the lettuce, scallions, and the bouquet garni tied in cheesecloth or placed in a tea infuser.
4. Simmer the ingredients, covered, for 25 minutes.
5. Drain the vegetables in a colander over a bowl, reserving the cooking water.
6. Over another bowl work the lettuce-pea pod mixture through the fine disc of a food mill.
7. In a large saucepan over low heat, melt the butter, adding the flour and whisking it into a roux for a few seconds.
8. Add the cream, whisking constantly.
9. Immediately add 1 cup of reserved cooking water, and whisk 2 – 3 minutes as the mixture thickens.
10. Add the pea-lettuce purée and salt to the saucepan.
11. Don't boil the soup, but reheat it for 2 – 3 minutes.

Serves 4

Vegetable and Legume

Peanut Soup

Peanuts aren't really nuts but are more related to pea pods that form underground. This is a soup most children will enjoy if they like peanut butter.

3 C vegetable stock
1 small ripe banana, peeled
5 T smooth peanut butter (natural)
2 T cold water

1 T cornstarch
¼ t salt
1 t lemon juice
Sprinkle of turmeric

1. In a large saucepan over medium heat, bring the stock to a simmer.
2. Slice the banana into the container of a blender, and purée it well for 1 minute.
3. Whisk this purée into the hot stock.
4. Whisk the peanut butter a tablespoon at a time into the stock.
5. In a measuring cup, mix the water and cornstarch. Stir this mixture into the soup, and simmer the soup for 2 – 3 minutes, stirring constantly, until it thickens.
6. Add the salt, lemon juice, and turmeric.

Serves 4

PIMENTO SOUP

This soup has an almond undertaste, but the sweet red pepper definitely predominates. As tempting as it might be to use a blender or food processor in this recipe, don't. The soup will turn out tasting like a sandbox special.

24 whole almonds, blanched
2 T olive oil
4 whole prepared pimentos, rinsed and drained
4 peppercorns
3 garlic cloves, peeled, crushed, and minced

1 t parsley, de-stemmed and minced
1 t saffron threads
2 ½ C boiling water
2 slices French or Italian bread (a day old), cut into 1-inch squares and toasted in the oven

1. To blanch the almonds, drop them in boiling water for 2 minutes, and then run cold water over them. Slip off the skins by holding the almond at the base with your thumb and index finger and press.
2. Halve the almonds. Dry them on paper towels. In a skillet over medium heat, sauté them in the oil until they are a dark golden color on both sides. Remove them to a bowl with a slotted spoon.
3. Add the pimentos, peppercorns, garlic, parsley, and saffron to the same oil over medium heat. Stir and sauté them for 5 minutes.
4. In a mortar, pound the ingredients with a pestle until they make a fine paste. This also may be done by passing the ingredients through the fine disc of a food mill into a bowl and then mashing them into a smooth paste with the back of a wooden spoon.
5. Place this mixture in a saucepan. When you're ready to eat, pour the boiling water over the mixture and stir it. Keep the soup on a hot burner until ready to serve. Place a few French bread croutons in each bowl and pour the soup over them.

Serves 4 small portions

VEGETABLE AND LEGUME

Pine Nut Soup

This soup is unusual, creamy, and distinctive. Pine nuts come from the cone of a special pine. They are collected by Native Americans in this country. In Spain they're called piñons and in Italy, pignoli.

1 T olive oil	1 C pine nuts
1 T sweet butter	¼ t salt
⅓ C onion, peeled and diced	3 T heavy cream
2¼ C vegetable stock	Sprinkle of mace

1. Heat the oil and butter in a large saucepan over medium heat. Add the onion, cover, and sweat for 5 – 8 minutes, stirring occasionally to prevent browning.
2. Add the stock, pine nuts, and salt. Cover and boil gently for 30 minutes.
3. Pour the pine nut mixture into a blender and blend for 1 minute. Return the purée to the rinsed saucepan and whisk in the cream.
4. Heat the soup but don't boil it. Sprinkle each serving with mace.

Serves 4

Quick Tomato Soup

For those who "put up" garden tomatoes or freeze them, this is a special soup in winter as well as summer. The recipe may be doubled, tripled, and quadrupled for extra diners.

2 C tomatoes, peeled, cored, and chopped	2 – 3 T milk
	¼ t salt
1 T sour cream	Sprinkle of imported oregano

1. In a small saucepan over medium heat, cook the tomatoes for 10 minutes.
2. Place them in a strainer over a bowl, and with a wooden spoon mash the tomato pulp through. Discard the residue and seeds.
3. Pour the tomato sauce from the bowl into the rinsed saucepan, and bring it to a simmer for 2 – 3 minutes.
4. Whisk in the sour cream and milk to the desired consistency. Add salt and oregano, and stir it in while heating the soup 2 – 3 minutes.

Serves 2

Savoy Cabbage and Lentil Dal

Dal is a spicy, thick, East Indian dish. This is a version of a dal recommended by Julie Jordan, our friend and author of the vegetarian Cabbagetown Café Cookbook. We have placed less emphasis on "spicy." Savoy cabbage is the king of cabbages because of its buttery texture.

1 C orange lentils
5 C water
¼ C safflower oil
2 t mustard seeds
1 C onion, peeled and chopped
2 C savoy cabbage, finely shredded
1 t cumin

1 t coriander
1 t turmeric
1 garlic clove, peeled, crushed, and minced
3 C tomatoes, peeled, with juice
1 t salt
¼ t ground red pepper (cayenne)
1 T lemon juice

1. Wash and rinse the lentils. Place them in a large saucepan with 3 cups water, boil, cover, and simmer 15 minutes. Remove from the burner.
2. Meanwhile, in a heavy Dutch oven or soup pot over a high burner, heat the oil.
3. Add the mustard seeds to the hot oil. When they swirl and darken (about 2–3 minutes), add the onion and cabbage and sauté them 2–3 minutes. Reduce the heat to medium.
4. Add the cumin, coriander, turmeric, and garlic. Sweat the cabbage, covered, for 5–8 minutes, stirring occasionally so it doesn't brown.
5. Add the tomatoes. Bring them to a boil over high heat. Lower the heat, and simmer the vegetables for 45 minutes.
6. Add the salt, cayenne pepper, remaining 2 cups of water, the cooked lentils, and lemon juice. Boil the soup 10 minutes.

Serves 6

VEGETABLE AND LEGUME

SAVOY CABBAGE SOUP

The outer leaves of savoy cabbage usually are greener than regular cabbage. It also has a milder flavor. All cabbages are high in vitamin A, calcium, and vitamin C, making a nutritionally rich soup.

2 rashers lean bacon, diced
1 T safflower oil
2 C savoy cabbage, finely shredded
1 leek (white part only), well washed and sliced into ½-inch rounds
3 C water
½ t salt
1 C milk
½ C heavy cream
Sprinkle of white pepper

1. In a heavy soup pot over medium-high heat, fry the bacon in the oil.
2. Add the cabbage and leeks and sauté them 2 – 3 minutes.
3. Add the water and salt. Bring the liquid to a boil.
4. Cover and simmer the ingredients for 45 minutes.
5. Add the milk, cream, and pepper to the vegetables. Heat but don't boil the soup.

Serves 4

SEMOLINA SOUP

Semolina is a granular durhum wheat, yellow in color and resembling cornmeal. It is the basis for most pastas. In this soup semolina acts as a thickening agent.

⅓ C semolina
3 T olive oil
½ C onion, peeled and diced
¼ C celery, threaded and thinly sliced
½ C carrots, scraped and thinly sliced
½ C turnip, peeled and chopped
4 C vegetable stock
¼ t fresh tarragon leaves, minced
½ t salt

1. In a heavy skillet over medium-high heat, toast the semolina, stirring it constantly with a wooden spoon until it turns golden. Set it aside.
2. In a heavy saucepan, heat the olive oil. Add the onion and celery and sauté them 2 – 3 minutes. Cover and let them sweat for 5 – 8 minutes, stirring occasionally.

3. Add the carrots and turnips to the onion and celery mixture. Cover and sweat another 5 – 8 minutes, stirring occasionally.
4. Add the stock and tarragon. Stir the semolina into the stock. Cover and simmer the soup for 30 minutes. Stir in the salt.

Serves 4

ᘒ
SOUPE AUX HERBES FINES

What could be simpler? We mince our herbs by bunching the tops and snipping them finely with kitchen shears. Only fresh herbs will do for this fast and delicious panacea. The soup may be served chilled — reduce the butter to 1 tablespoon, let it cool, and refrigerate for 2 hours.

2 T sweet butter
1 T fresh chives, minced
1 T fresh parsley, de-stemmed
 and minced
1 T fresh dill, minced

1 T fresh tarragon leaves,
 minced
3 C buttermilk
1 C heavy cream
½ t salt
Sprinkle of white pepper

1. In a soup pot over medium heat, melt the butter.
2. Add the chives, parsley, dill, and tarragon. Sauté them 1 minute.
3. Add the buttermilk and cream. Heat but do not boil.
4. Stir in the salt and pepper.

Serves 4

ᘒ
SOYBEAN SOUP

Use precooked, toasted soy grits in this fast-cooking vegetable soup. Soybeans are extremely high in protein, and in the grit form they cook fast.

2 T olive oil
½ C onion, peeled and diced
1 garlic clove, peeled, crushed,
 and minced
4 C vegetable stock
½ C carrots, scraped and diced
½ C celery, threaded and diced
½ C turnips, peeled and chopped
 bite-size

½ C potatoes, peeled and
 chopped bite-size
¼ C parsley, de-stemmed and
 minced
1 t fresh tarragon leaves, minced
¼ C soy grits
½ t salt
Freshly ground black pepper

1. In a soup pot, heat the oil and sauté the onion and garlic a few seconds. Cover and let them sweat for 5–8 minutes, stirring occasionally.
2. Add the stock, carrots, celery, turnips, potatoes, parsley, tarragon, and grits to the pot. Cover and simmer for 30 minutes.
3. Add salt and pepper.

Serves 4

&

SPAGHETTI SQUASH SOUP

Spaghetti squash is a magical vegetable that really does look like spaghetti after it's cooked. This vegetarian fare is filling and different. Children espe-cially will be enticed to eat their squash prepared this way.

1 lb spaghetti squash	2 C whole peeled tomatoes, with
4 T olive oil	juice
1 garlic clove, peeled, crushed,	¼ C red wine
and minced	1 T tomato paste
2 T parsley, de-stemmed and	3 C water
minced	1 t salt
2 T onion, peeled and diced	Freshly ground black pepper
⅛ t imported oregano	Freshly grated Parmesan or
	Romano cheese

1. Cut the squash in half lengthwise, and remove the seeds with a spoon. Place the inner sides down on a foil-covered baking sheet, and bake the squash 1 hour at 350° F.
2. In a soup pot heat the oil, and sauté the garlic, parsley, onion, and oregano a few minutes. Cover and sweat another 5–8 minutes, stirring occasionally.
3. Add the tomatoes, red wine, and tomato paste. Simmer, covered, over medium-low heat for 20 minutes.
4. Meanwhile, with a fork remove the squash strands from the skin.
5. Add the squash, water, salt, and pepper to the soup.
6. Simmer the soup another 15 minutes. Place a bowl of Parmesan cheese on the table.

Serves 4

SPINACH GNOCCHI SOUP

Leftover gnocchi freeze well for future use. These delicious spinach dumplings may be reheated and served with sweet butter and Parmesan as a side dish to an Italian meal.

10 ozs fresh spinach
¼ C water
½ C ricotta
1 egg, slightly beaten

**1 C freshly grated Parmesan
  cheese**
⅛ t freshly grated nutmeg
Flour as needed
8 C vegetable stock

1. Prepare the spinach by washing the leaves and removing the stalks and center ribs. Place the leaves in a large pot with the water, and steam them for 5–8 minutes. They should be wilted and soft.
2. Pour the spinach into a strainer, and press on it with a wooden spoon to squeeze out all the water. Pour out the water. Chop the spinach with a knife or mezza luna.
3. In a large bowl mix the chopped spinach, ricotta, egg, Parmesan, and nutmeg. Turn the dough onto a well-floured board, and form it into a ball. Let it stand for 20–30 minutes.
4. Shape the gnocchi into small oblong rolls 1–inch in diameter. Roll each lightly in flour.
5. In a large skillet bring the stock to a boil, reduce the heat to a simmer, and add the gnocchi. Cook them for 3–4 minutes, but do not boil the stock. When they're ready, they'll float to the top.
6. Remove them with a slotted spoon, and place a few of the gnocchi in each bowl. Ladle stock over them.

Serves 6–8

VEGETABLE AND LEGUME

SPINACH SOUP

This soup combines the tastes of spinach salad with the texture of cream of spinach soup. Croutons may be added too.

2 rashers bacon, diced
1 T olive oil
10 ozs fresh spinach
3⅓ C milk
3 T flour

Freshly grated nutmeg
Sprinkle of white pepper
½ t salt
2 hard-boiled eggs, peeled

1. In a soup pot over medium heat, fry the bacon in the olive oil. Drain off the excess oil, and reserve the bacon bits in the pot.
2. Wash the spinach well. Remove the central ribs and stems. Pile the leaves one on top of the other, fold them in half, and with a sharp knife, cut the leaves into thin strips.
3. Add the spinach to the bacon in the soup pot over low heat. Cover the pot, and simmer the spinach for 8–10 minutes, stirring at intervals to make sure the spinach doesn't adhere to the pan. If so, add a little water.
4. When the spinach has wilted, add 3 cups of milk, and heat the soup to scalding but don't boil it.
5. In a small bowl mix the flour into the remaining ⅓ cup of milk to form a smooth paste.
6. Whisk this paste into the soup, and continue whisking until the soup thickens. Simmer for 5 minutes, stirring occasionally.
7. Add the nutmeg, white pepper, and salt.
8. Chop the hard-boiled eggs, and serve a tablespoon of the egg garnish on top of each serving.

Serves 4

ॐ

SPLIT PEA SOUP

*This dish is almost too easy, and that's why it heads the list of favorites,
especially in winter. As they say, it sticks to your ribs.*

2½ C split peas
6½ C water
½ lb smoked ham hock or
   Canadian bacon
1 T celery leaves, minced

½ t thyme
⅓ C onion, peeled and diced
½ C carrots, scraped and diced
½ t salt
Freshly ground black pepper

1. Place all the ingredients in a large pot or Dutch oven. Bring the liquid
   to a boil, reduce the heat, and simmer for 45 minutes. Stir occasionally,
   and add water if the soup thickens too much.
2. Remove the ham hock, cut off the ham, and return it to the soup.
   Discard the bone.

Serves 4–6

ॐ

STRING BEAN SOUP

*String beans are as basic as bread, but dressed up in this soup they take on
a new dimension. Be sure to use the freshest, thinnest beans available. Most
beans grown commercially these days are stringless.*

2 T olive oil
½ C onion, peeled and chopped
¼ t fresh tarragon leaves,
   minced
2 C water

1½ C string beans (about ½ lb),
   ends trimmed and snapped
   into bite-size pieces
½ t salt
1 T flour
1 C sour cream

1. In a large saucepan over a medium burner, heat the oil and sauté the
   onion and tarragon 2–3 minutes. Cover and let them sweat 5–8 minutes.
2. Add the water, beans, and salt. Bring to a boil, cover, and continue
   boiling gently for 15 minutes.
3. In a small mixing bowl, blend the flour into the sour cream. Remove ¼
   cup of the bean liquid, and stir it into the sour cream mixture. Mix the
   sour cream mixture into the soup. Bring it to a simmer for 2 minutes,
   stirring continually.

Serves 4

VEGETABLE AND LEGUME

SUCCOTASH SOUP

Succotash is a shortened form of the native American word misickquastash, *which refers to kernels of corn on the cob. Garden-fresh vegetables always taste best. Red sweet pepper is the matured version of the familiar green bell pepper.*

1 C baby lima beans
Water
3 T corn oil
1 C corn, cut from cob
¼ C sweet green bell pepper,
   cored, seeded, and diced

¼ C sweet red bell pepper,
   cored, seeded, and diced
3½ C milk
3 T flour
½ t salt

1. In a small saucepan, cover the lima beans with water. Over medium heat simmer them, covered, for 15 minutes.
2. Heat the oil in a heavy skillet, and add the corn and peppers. Stir-fry over medium-low heat for 2 minutes. Cover and let them sweat 2 – 3 minutes. Remove them with a slotted spoon, and place them in a soup pot.
3. Drain the lima beans, and place them in the pot with the corn and peppers.
4. Add 3 cups of milk, and bring it just below a boil over medium heat.
5. In a small bowl mix the flour and remaining ½ cup of milk into a smooth paste.
6. Add this thickening to the soup. Whisk until the soup thickens.
7. Stir in the salt.

Serves 4 – 6

SUNFLOWER SEED AND CHARD SOUP

This soup has a forest green color and nutty undertaste. The seeds are high in protein, and chard is a good source of calcium. Rhubarb chard may be substituted. The center ribs and stems should be removed from both green and red Swiss chard for this soup. They may be cooked separately, diced, and creamed like asparagus as a side dish for another meal.

1 C sunflower seeds, toasted
2 T olive oil
½ C onion, peeled and diced
1 garlic clove, peeled, crushed,
   and minced
3 C vegetable stock

3 C Swiss chard leaves, de-
   stemmed and shredded
1 t fresh tarragon leaves, minced
¾ t salt
Freshly ground black pepper

1. Toast the seeds by placing them in a large iron skillet over high heat. Stir with a wooden spoon as they darken. Set them aside.
2. Heat the oil in a heavy soup pot over medium heat, sauté the onion and garlic briefly, and cover them to sweat for 5–8 minutes.
3. Add the stock and chard. Bring them to a boil, cover, reduce the heat, and simmer for 15 minutes, stirring occasionally.
4. Add the seeds and tarragon. Simmer, covered, for 30 minutes.
5. Place (in 2 batches) in a blender and purée well. Return the purée to the rinsed saucepan, and add the salt and pepper to taste.

Serves 6

&

SWEET AND SOUR RED CABBAGE SOUP

This soup is cooked covered to retain the vitamins in the cabbage. The steps are simple, the color provocative, and the taste perfect to accompany a big loaf of pumpernickel bread.

3 T safflower oil
¼ C onion, peeled and chopped
2 C red cabbage, cored and
    shredded into fine slaw
½ C cooking apple, peeled,
    cored, and chopped

1 T tomato paste
5 C vegetable stock
1 T white vinegar
1 T honey
½ t salt

1. Heat the oil in a heavy soup pot over medium heat.
2. Add the onion and cabbage and sauté, stirring for 2–3 minutes.
3. Cover and sweat the onion and cabbage 5–8 minutes, stirring occasionally.
4. Add the apple, tomato paste, stock, vinegar, and honey. Simmer, covered, at a low boil for 1 ½ hours. Add the salt.

Serves 4

VEGETABLE AND LEGUME

SWISS CHARD SOUP

Older women need calcium to retain healthy bones. This soup is a good one to make a standard for that reason. Chard cooks fast compared with collard greens and kale, and it doesn't have the oxalic acid content that spinach does.

2 T safflower oil
1 garlic clove, peeled, crushed,
    and minced
½ C onion, peeled and chopped
3 C Swiss chard, de-stemmed
    and chopped

2 C vegetable stock
1 C milk
¼ t salt
Freshly ground black pepper

1. Place the oil in a heavy soup pot over medium heat. Sauté the garlic, onion, and chard for 2–3 minutes. (Be sure to remove the stem all the way up the leaf center.)
2. Cover and let the vegetables sweat for 5–8 minutes, stirring occasionally so they don't brown.
3. Add the stock and cook the chard ½ hour, adding extra stock if necessary.
4. Place the chard mixture in a blender with the milk and purée well.
5. Return the soup to the rinsed pot, heat, and stir in the salt and pepper to taste.

Serves 4

TOMATO MINT SOUP

The secret to this soup is to use vine-ripened tomatoes and fresh peppermint, both of which are easy to grow in your garden.

1 C celery, threaded and
    chopped
1 C carrots, scraped and
    chopped
2½ C water
2 C fresh tomatoes, peeled and
    cored (approximately 4–5
    tomatoes)

½ C onion, peeled and chopped
2 T olive oil
¼ C fresh mint leaves (reserve 4
    whole leaves as a garnish),
    minced
½ t salt

1. In a saucepan over medium heat, simmer the celery and carrots in the water for 10 minutes. Strain, reserving the liquid and discarding the vegetables.
2. Rinse the saucepan and add the tomatoes. Simmer them over medium heat for 10 minutes.
3. Meanwhile, sauté the onion in the oil for 2–3 minutes, cover, and let them sweat for 5–8 minutes, stirring occasionally.
4. Pour the tomatoes into a strainer over a bowl, and press the pulp with a wooden spoon. Discard the skins and seeds, but return the sauce to the pan.
5. Add the onion to the tomato sauce in the saucepan along with the mint and 1 cup of vegetable liquid. Simmer gently for 10 minutes. Cool.
6. Pour the soup into a blender and blend 1 minute. Return the purée to the saucepan and stir in the salt. Heat. Serve with a mint leaf garnish.

Serves 4

ॐ

Tomato Rice and Pine Nut Soup

More tomato flavor may be obtained by working the tomatoes through a food mill. The pine nuts are easily browned and toasted in a skillet over medium heat.

1½ T olive oil
¼ C onion, peeled and diced
4 large whole tomatoes
¼ t imported oregano

¼ t salt
¼ C cooked rice
1 T toasted pine nuts
2 T sour cream

1. Heat the oil in a heavy skillet and sauté the onion 2–3 minutes. Cover and sweat for 5–8 minutes, stirring occasionally.
2. Prepare the tomatoes by placing them in boiling water for a minute. Remove them to cold water. Peel off the broken skins, remove the core, and chop the tomatoes. Place them in a large saucepan, and boil them for 10 minutes.
3. Place the tomatoes and juice in a strainer over a bowl, and press the pulp and juice through with a wooden spoon to separate and remove the skin and seeds. Discard the pulp, and return the sauce in the bowl to the pan.
4. Add oregano, salt, cooked onion, rice, and pine nuts. Simmer 5 minutes until blended.
5. Whisk in the sour cream. Heat but do not boil.

Serves 4

TUNA SOUP

A dark, oily fish, fresh tuna is available at most fish markets and even local supermarkets. It definitely is worth a try if you're familiar with only canned tuna. Dill substitutes nicely for the tarragon in this quick, energy-providing soup.

3 T olive oil
1 garlic clove, peeled, crushed, and minced
¼ C onion, peeled and diced
1 T parsley, de-stemmed and minced
½ C celery, threaded and diced

⅛ t fresh tarragon leaves, minced
3½ C vegetable stock
1 C potatoes, peeled and chopped
½ lb fresh tuna, cut into bite-size pieces
1 C soft tofu, cut in bite-size dice
¼ t salt

1. Heat the oil in a large saucepan over medium heat. Add the garlic, onion, parsley, celery, and tarragon. Sauté 2–3 minutes. Cover and let the vegetables sweat 5–8 minutes.
2. Stir in the vegetable stock and bring it to a boil.
3. Add the potatoes and simmer them for 10 minutes.
4. Add the tuna and tofu. Simmer them for 2 minutes. Stir in the salt.

Serves 4

YELLOW SPLIT PEA AND HOMINY SOUP

Canadians use yellow peas so often that this is called Canadian Pea Soup. *It's a popular dish to serve after energetic wintertime sports. Hominy is whole kernel corn with the hulls removed. It comes in white and yellow and is canned in salt and water.*

1½ C yellow split peas
7–9 C water
1 smoked ham hock
1 T celery leaves, minced
½ C onion, peeled and diced

½ t thyme
Salt
Sprinkle of white pepper
14–16 oz prepared whole hominy (white or yellow)

1. Wash and drain the peas. In a large pot combine the water, ham hock, celery leaves, and onion.
2. Bring the water to a boil. Reduce the heat and boil slowly for 1 hour. If the soup is too thick, add water to desired consistency.

3. Season with thyme. Add salt and pepper to taste. (The ham hock will be salty, so taste the soup first.)
4. Drain and rinse the hominy and add it last. Heat the soup. If the meat on the ham hock is tender, cut pieces of ham into each serving bowl. Discard the bone.

Serves 4−6

ぴ
ZUCCHINI CELERY SOUP

This is another time-saver worth remembering. Make sure the celery is threaded and fresh.

2 C water	**1½ C zucchini, thinly sliced**
1 C celery, threaded and diced	**½ C milk**
1 t fennel seeds in cheesecloth or	**¼ C sour cream**
a tea infuser	**¾ t salt**
2 T olive oil	

1. In a large saucepan over high heat, bring the water to a boil. Add the celery and bouquet garni of fennel seeds. Lower the heat and simmer for 20 minutes.
2. Remove and discard the fennel seed bouquet garni.
3. In a skillet, heat the olive oil and sauté the zucchini for 3−5 minutes over medium heat.
4. Add the zucchini and leftover oil in the skillet to the celery mixture in the saucepan.
5. Stir in the milk and sour cream. Add the salt.
6. Bring the soup to a simmer but don't boil it.

Serves 4

VEGETABLE AND LEGUME

ZUCCHINI SOUP (CHILLED)

Zucchini is a favorite summer squash that adds a cool, green shade to any summer meal.

1 C celery, threaded and
   chopped
1 C carrots, scraped and
   chopped
3 C water
3 C zucchini, chopped

3 fresh tarragon leaves, minced
¼ C leeks (white part only), well
   washed and diced
2 T olive oil
½ t salt
2 T sour cream

1. In a saucepan over high heat, boil the celery and carrots in the water for 10 minutes. Drain, reserving the liquid and discarding the vegetables.
2. Return the vegetable liquid to the saucepan, and add the zucchini and tarragon. Boil gently for 10 minutes.
3. Meanwhile, in a skillet over medium heat sauté the leeks in the oil, cover, and sweat them for 5–8 minutes.
4. Place the leeks in a blender container. Pour the cooked zucchini and vegetable water into the blender with the leeks and blend 1 minute. Pour the purée into a bowl.
5. Stir in the salt and sour cream, using a whisk to blend well.
6. This soup tastes equally delicious hot or refrigerated for a few hours.

Serves 4

Pickled Onions

SOUPS

FRUIT AND NUT

*Most of the following soups are served chilled
and are not based on a stock*

SOUPS
182

Apricot Soup (Chilled)

Velvety and light, this makes a fitting choice to begin or end a luncheon on a sultry summer day.

1 C dried apricots
Water (at least 3 C)
6 T sugar

1 t fresh lemon juice
Sprinkle of allspice
⅔ C heavy cream

1. In a small saucepan, cover the apricots with water. Rehydrate them by bringing the water to a boil, covering the pan, and turning off the heat. Let the apricots soak for 30 minutes.
2. Drain the apricots and reserve 1 ½ cups of the cooking liquid.
3. Place the liquid in a saucepan. Add the sugar and lemon juice, and bring the liquid to a boil for a few minutes. Take the pan off the burner, and let the mixture cool.
4. Place the liquid in a blender. Add the apricots and allspice. Blend for 2 minutes. Pour the purée into a container, and let it cool to room temperature.
5. In a separate bowl whip the cream and fold it into the soup. Refrigerate for at least 1 hour.
6. Serve in chilled glass bowls or punch cups.

Serves 4

Apricot Yogurt Soup (Chilled)

Try this for breakfast or as a creamy orange-colored dessert. Dried apricots, rehydrated and cooked until soft, also may be used in this recipe.

2 C canned apricots (or very ripe
**   fresh apricots), seeded**
½ C apricot nectar

½ C apple juice
1 C plain yogurt
1 T grated coconut

1. Place the apricots in a blender. (If the apricots are canned, they should be drained first.)
2. Add the apricot nectar and apple juice and blend well 1 minute.
3. Pour the purée into a bowl and whisk in the yogurt.
4. Chill for at least 30 minutes. Sprinkle each portion with grated coconut.

Serves 4

Fruit and Nut

❧
BANANA RUM SOUP (CHILLED)

For those who like the taste and texture of buttermilk, this thick tropical soup provides a treat.

⅔ C buttermilk
½ C plain yogurt
2 C ripe bananas (2–3 bananas),
    sliced

2 T dark rum
2 T dark brown sugar
¼ t allspice

1. Place all the ingredients in a blender. Purée for 1 minute.
2. Refrigerate for 30 minutes or more.

Serves 4

❧
BEET AND CHERRY
SOUP (CHILLED)

This clear fruit soup has an exquisite magenta color and a beguiling, almost undetectable beet flavor. When peeling raw beets, keep them in a stainless steel bowl or sink since they stain. Of course, cooked fresh sweet cherries would be superb in this soup.

4 C beets, well washed, de-
    stemmed, peeled, and grated (or
    shredded in a food processor)
4 C water
¼ C fresh lemon juice
Sprinkle of allspice

¼ C sugar
2 T cornstarch
¼ C cold water
1 C prepared pitted sweet cher-
    ries, drained and halved.
¼ C sour cream

1. In a large saucepan, boil the shredded beets in the water and lemon juice for 15 minutes.
2. Pour the beets and water into a strainer or colander placed over a large bowl. Press the beets with a stainless steel spoon to extract the juice. Discard the beets in the strainer.
3. Return the beet juice to the rinsed saucepan, and add the allspice and sugar. Reheat the liquid to a boil.
4. Dissolve the cornstarch in the cold water. Pour it into the beets and stir the liquid. Boil gently for 1 minute.
5. Remove the pan from the heat. Add the pitted cherries to the clear beet soup. Cool it to room temperature before refrigerating it for at least 2 hours.
6. Crown each serving with a tablespoon of sour cream.

Serves 4

Black Currant and Apple Soup (Chilled)

This is a mellow blend of dark flavors, especially enjoyable as a postlude to a light lunch.

1 C dried black currants
½ C cassis (a currant-based liqueur)
1 C apples, peeled and cored (2 small apples), grated
3 C water

3 T brown sugar
⅛ t allspice
1 t fresh lemon juice
2 T cornstarch
¼ C cold water
¼ C sour cream

1. Place the black currants in a large saucepan, and add the cassis. Bring them to a low boil, cover, and simmer them for 10 minutes. This will plump the currants.
2. Add the apples and water and boil them for 15 minutes.
3. Pour the contents into a sieve or colander placed over a large bowl to retain the liquid. Press on the apples and currants with a wooden spoon to extract the juice. Discard the apples and currants. Return the liquid to the rinsed saucepan.
4. Add the sugar, allspice, and lemon juice. Bring them to a simmer to dissolve the sugar.
5. In a measuring cup mix the cornstarch in the cold water. Pour this mixture into the soup, and bring the soup to a low boil for 2 minutes, stirring until the soup clears and thickens.
6. Cool to room temperature, and refrigerate at least 2 hours.
7. Add a tablespoon of sour cream to each serving bowl.

Serves 4

FRUIT AND NUT

Blueberry Soup (Chilled)

Of course, fresh blueberries are best. Uncultivated berries tend to be winey and may need more sugar. This soup tastes as sumptuous and royal as its color. Again, blueberries stain, so be sure to use stainless steel utensils and pots.

**4 C fresh or frozen blueberries,
  de-stemmed
2 C water
3 T sugar**

**1 T cornstarch
¼ C cold water
½ t almond extract**

1. In a large stainless steel saucepan, boil the blueberries in the water until they are soft, approximately 5 – 8 minutes. Keep the blueberries in a low boil and the saucepan covered to prevent splattering.
2. Pour the blueberries into a sieve or colander placed over a large bowl. Press on the blueberries with a wooden spoon to extract *only* the juice. Discard the blueberries.
3. Pour the blueberry liquid back into the rinsed saucepan, and reheat it to a simmer.
4. Add the sugar, stirring to dissolve it.
5. In a measuring cup, dissolve the cornstarch in the cold water. Pour this mixture into the blueberry liquid, stirring constantly.
6. Bring the soup to a low boil, and stir 2 – 3 minutes until the soup thickens and clears.
7. Stir in the almond extract. Cool the soup to room temperature, and refrigerate at least 2 hours.
8. Before serving, whip the cream, adding the sugar as you whip it. Swirl a mound of whipped cream on top of each bowl.

Serves 4

Brazilian Vitamina
Soup (Chilled)

Brazilians resort to vitaminas *at all times of the day. Drink this from a mug for breakfast, or serve it in a cut-glass bowl as a soup. The fruits should be fresh, ripe, and seasonal. If strawberries aren't available, substitute nutritionally rich kiwis. (One combination Brazilians avoid is papaya and milk, which does not blend well in the stomach.)*

1 large mango, peeled, seeded,
and sliced
1 C banana, peeled and sliced
1 C fresh strawberries, hulled

1 C avocado, peeled, seeded, and
sliced
2 C lemon-flavored yogurt
1 C milk
¼ C sugar

1. Place all ingredients in a blender and purée for 2 minutes. Refrigerate for 30 minutes or eat right away.

Serves 6

Butter Pecan Soup (Chilled)

The pecans should be fresh. Fortunately, we have a relative in Alabama who keeps us supplied. The soup is rich; serve it in small chilled bowls.

1 T sweet butter
1½ T flour
1 C milk
1 T light brown sugar

1 C pecan meats
2 egg yolks
1 C heavy cream
1 T dark rum

1. In a saucepan over medium heat, melt the butter.
2. Add the flour and make a roux, whisking well.
3. Add the milk ½ cup at a time, whisking as the mixture thickens.
4. Remove the mixture from the burner and stir in the sugar.
5. Place the pecan meats in a food processor or blender. Turn on high for a second and then off. Do this 10–12 times. Don't purée them. Grind them finely.
6. Add the pecans to the white sauce mixture, and simmer them for 2–3 minutes over medium-low heat, whisking occasionally.
7. Whisk the egg yolks into the cream, and add them to the soup. Add the rum.

8. Simmer the soup at just below a boil for 10 minutes, whisking constantly.
9. Remove the soup from the heat, and cool it in a covered container.
10. Refrigerate it for 3 hours before serving. Whisk the soup well if a crust forms.

Serves 4

⊱

BUTTERMILK WALNUT
SOUP (CHILLED)

A simple, quick soup to prepare, this taste treat is tangy and refreshing in midsummer. Keep the servings small as a singular tongue-teaser for the entrée.

2 T olive oil
¼ t salt
2 C buttermilk

2 t scallions (white part only), minced
6 T walnuts, finely ground (reserve 4 walnut halves)

1. In a bowl, stir together the oil, salt, and buttermilk.
2. Mix in the scallions.
3. In a blender or food processor, grind the walnuts 2–3 minutes until they're a fine powder.
4. Stir the walnut powder into the buttermilk mixture, and refrigerate the soup for 2–3 hours.
5. Serve in chilled bowls, placing a walnut half in the center of each serving.

Serves 4

⊱

CHOCOLATE MINT SOUP (CHILLED)

It doesn't take much to turn a favorite hot drink into a cold dessert soup that is absolutely tantalizing.

¼ C cocoa
½ C boiling water
1⅓ C evaporated milk
10 fresh mint leaves

¼ C sugar
⅛ t ground cinnamon
⅔ C heavy cream
4 mint leaves

1. Place the cocoa in a medium-size saucepan. Add 3 tablespoons of boiling water, and stir it into a paste. Pour in the rest of the water. Add the evaporated milk, mint leaves, sugar, and cinnamon. Bring the mixture to a boil over medium heat, and simmer the soup for 5 minutes.
2. With a slotted spoon remove the mint leaves and discard them. Remove the saucepan from the heat.
3. Stir in the cream. Return the soup to the burner, and bring it to the simmering point. Do not boil. Cool to room temperature. Pour it into a covered container, and refrigerate the soup at least 2 hours.
4. Immediately before serving, stir the soup to dissolve any crust that may have formed on top. Float a fresh mint leaf on each serving.

Serves 4

&

CIDER SOUP (CHILLED)

The quality of cider varies with the types of apples pressed. If possible, locate cider from an orchard with a wide variety of old-time apple trees like Sheep Nose and antique Rhode Island Greening, which make the most flavorful soup.

2 C water
3 C cooking apples (about 4 apples), peeled, cored, and sliced (try Northern Spy, Jonathan, Cortland, Rome Beauty, or Rhode Island Greening apples)

3 T dark brown sugar
¼ t allspice
1 ¼ C apple cider
1 T fresh lemon juice
1 T cornstarch
¼ C heavy cream

1. Place the water and apples in a large saucepan. Bring the water to a boil, and cook the apples for 10 – 15 minutes until they're soft.
2. Pour them into a sieve or colander placed over a large bowl to catch the juice. Press the apples with a wooden spoon to extract all the juice. Discard the pulp.
3. Return the juice to the rinsed saucepan. Add the sugar, allspice, 1 cup of cider, and the lemon juice.
4. Simmer the liquid over moderate heat, and stir to dissolve the sugar.
5. In a measuring cup, mix the cornstarch with remaining ¼ cup of cold cider. Stir this mixture into the hot cider mixture, and bring them to a boil. Gently boil for 2 – 3 minutes while stirring occasionally until the soup thickens and clears.
6. Remove the soup from the burner, and cool it to room temperature. Refrigerate it for at least 2 hours.
7. Pour a little cream into each serving.

Serves 4

FRUIT AND NUT

189

Coco Loco Soup (Chilled)

This soup has a distinctive tropical punch to it. Canned coconut milk and pineapple may be substituted, although concocting the soup from fresh fruits heightens the taste and reinforces the enjoyment of creating a stunning soup from scratch.

1 whole fresh coconut
2 C fresh pineapple, peeled,
   cored, and chopped

¼ C confectioners' sugar
3 T dark rum

1. Drill a hole in one of the "eyes" at the end of the coconut (or hammer a large nail into one).
2. Drain the liquid from the nut and reserve it in a bowl.
3. Split the coconut with a hammer or hatchet. Remove the coconut meat (a screwdriver may be used to pry it loose). Peel off the thin, dark rind on the meat. Wash the coconut meat.
4. Drop small chunks of the coconut meat into an operating food processor to grate it. Set it aside.
5. Mix 1 ½ cups of grated coconut with 1 ½ cups of coconut milk in a blender. Blend 2–3 minutes.
6. Place the coconut in a strainer over a large bowl, and with a wooden spoon, press on the grated coconut. Reserve the coconut milk in the bowl.
7. Place the pineapple and 1 cup of this coconut milk in a blender. Blend for 2 minutes. Remove the soup to a mixing bowl.
8. Sift the confectioners' sugar into the soup. Stir in the rum. Refrigerate the soup for at least 30 minutes.

Serves 4–6

CRANBERRY SOUP (CHILLED)

Cranberries are an American fruit high in vitamin C. They come into season in the late fall and freeze well. This soup is sweet and rich, and the whipped cream cuts the edge on the berries. Chicken and turkey dinners gain an entirely new perspective when accompanied by this delicious soup.

4 C fresh or frozen cranberries, de-stemmed
3 C water
1 cinnamon stick
1¼ C sugar
1 t grated fresh orange peel

1 T cornstarch
2 T orange juice
¼ C cranberry liqueur (or cassis)
½ C heavy cream
2 t confectioners' sugar
Whipped cream

1. Place the cranberries, water, cinnamon stick, sugar, and orange peel in a large saucepan, and bring them to a boil over medium heat. Boil the berries about 10 minutes or until they have "popped" and softened. Taste the cranberry mixture for sugar. Remember that a sweet liqueur will be added later.
2. Strain the juice into a bowl, gently pressing on the berries in the strainer to extract the liquid.
3. Return the liquid to the rinsed pan and bring it to a boil.
4. In a measuring cup, blend the cornstarch with the orange juice and add it to the soup, stirring constantly.
5. Simmer and stir the soup 2–3 minutes until it thickens and clears. Remove the cinnamon stick.
6. Cool the soup to room temperature, and refrigerate it for at least 2 hours.
7. Stir in the liqueur.
8. Whip the cream, slowly adding the confectioners' sugar as you whip.
9. To each serving add a dollop of whipped cream.

Serves 6

FRUIT AND NUT

CREAM OF BANANA AND ALMOND SOUP (CHILLED)

Bananas have a strong flavor, so judge the number of bananas used according to taste and size.

¼ C almonds, blanched and
   finely ground
2 C milk

2 C bananas (3–4 small
   bananas), peeled and sliced
2 T sugar
½ C heavy cream

1. Place all the ingredients in a blender, and blend well for 2 minutes.
2. Refrigerate at least 30 minutes. Serve in chilled cups or bowls.

Serves 4

EGGNOG APPLE SOUP (CHILLED)

Commercial eggnog usually is in season from Thanksgiving through New Year's, or you may make your own eggnog. Add this easy soup to a festive buffet or après-ski banquet.

2 Northern Spy or other cooking
   apples, cored and quartered
2 Granny Smith apples, cored
   and quartered
2 C apple juice

1 cinnamon stick
½ C brown sugar
3 C eggnog
Freshly grated nutmeg
¼ C rum

1. In a large soup pot over medium-high heat, cook the apples in the apple juice with the cinnamon stick 10–15 minutes until they're soft.
2. Remove the cinnamon stick. Then with a fine disc in place, pass the apples through a food mill. This yields about 4 cups of sauce.
3. Dissolve the sugar in the hot sauce, stirring well. Cool the sauce. Add the eggnog, nutmeg, and rum.
4. Refrigerate at least 2 hours.

Serves 6–8

Fig Soup (Chilled)

Preserved semidried figs are sugary and rich, so small portions of this soup are better. The sour cream cuts the potency of this strong but tasty fruit.

1 C (about ½ lb) Calimyrna figs
or other light-colored preserved figs
2½ C water
½ C sweet white wine

⅔ C apple, peeled, cored, and
chopped
Sprinkle of ground cloves
1 T sugar
4 t sour cream

1. Cut the figs into small pieces, and place them in a large saucepan with the water and wine.
2. Over medium heat, bring the liquid to a boil and cover the pan. Simmer the figs and apples for 20–30 minutes until they soften.
3. Place the figs and apples with the cloves and sugar in a blender container, and blend for 2 minutes.
4. Return the purée to the rinsed saucepan, and bring it to a boil for a few minutes, stirring to dissolve the sugar.
5. Pour the soup through a strainer into a bowl, pressing it through with a spoon in order to strain out the small fig seeds. Discard the seeds.
6. Cool the soup to room temperature, and refrigerate it for 2 hours or more.
7. Add a teaspoon of sour cream to each portion.

Serves 4

Kiwi Soup (Chilled)

Fresh kiwis and bananas should not be stored in the refrigerator. They are picked green, so they probably will take 3–4 days to ripen at room temperature. This is a fast, fresh dessert soup extra high in vitamin C and calcium.

4 large kiwis, peeled
1 banana, peeled
1 C fresh orange juice

1 C lemon-flavored yogurt
3 T sugar

1. Place all ingredients in a blender and blend for 2 minutes.
2. Eat at room temperature or refrigerate for 30 minutes.

Serves 4

FRUIT AND NUT

193

LITCHI WATERMELON
SOUP (CHILLED)

Litchi (or lychee) is a Chinese fruit that grows on a small tree. It has a soft shell and may be fresh, preserved, or canned. Litchis now are grown in the United States. This is one of our favorite culinary experiments. It is simple to prepare, adventurous, and tastes like ambrosia.

4 ½ – 5 C watermelon, rind
   removed, seeded, and cut in
   chunks
1 T cornstarch

1 T cold water
1 t sugar
16 – 20 litchi fruit (a 15-oz can)

1. Place the watermelon chunks in a food processor or blender and purée for 1 minute.
2. Pour the watermelon into a sieve over a bowl and reserve the juice. Discard any pulp left in the sieve.
3. Place 2 cups of watermelon juice in a saucepan over medium heat. Bring it to a boil.
4. In a measuring cup dissolve the cornstarch in the cold water, and stir this mixture into the boiling juice.
5. Simmer and stir the soup 2 – 3 minutes until it clears and thickens.
6. Stir in the sugar.
7. Cool the soup to room temperature.
8. Drain the litchis and place them in a bowl in the refrigerator. Also refrigerate the soup for 2 hours.
9. Before serving, cut 2 litchis in half and reserve them. Place the remaining litchis and the watermelon soup in a blender. Purée them for 1 minute or until smooth.
10. Garnish each serving with half a litchi.

Serves 4

SOUPS

LOVE APPLE SOUP (CHILLED)

This cocktail-style soup whets the appetite and isn't as strong as the usual drinks served before dinner.

2 C fresh orange juice, strained
2 C prepared tomato-vegetable
   juice
6 drops Tabasco sauce
1 t sugar

Salt
1 jigger vodka (1 ½ oz)
2 T parsley, de-stemmed and
   minced

1. Mix the orange juice, tomato-vegetable juice, Tabasco sauce, sugar, and salt to taste.
2. Chill well. Immediately before serving, add the vodka and a sprinkle of parsley on each serving.

Serves 4

MELON MANGO SOUP (CHILLED)

The summery pastels of orange melon and mango dotted with pale lime green honeydew please the eye, and the bubbly champagne adds a light sparkle to any summer meal.

3 C cantaloupe, rind removed,
   diced
1½ – 2 C ripe mango, peeled and
   sliced from the seed

2 T fresh lime juice
1 C brut champagne or dry
   sparkling white wine
1 C small honeydew melon balls

1. Purée the cantaloupe and mango in a blender or food processor for a few minutes.
2. Add the lime juice to the puréed fruit and stir it in.
3. Place the soup in a covered container, and refrigerate it for at least 2 hours.
4. Immediately before serving, uncork the champagne and pour it into the soup.
5. Garnish each portion with a few honeydew melon balls.

Serves 4

FRUIT AND NUT

195

Mint Tea Soup (Chilled)

Just about any herbal tea makes a thoroughly refreshing summer dessert soup. Try raspberry leaves or a combination of lemon- and orange-flavored infusions.

3 C water
¼ C dried spearmint leaves
3 T sugar

1½ T cornstarch
1 T cold water
2 lime slices

1. In a saucepan over high heat, bring the water to a boil.
2. Place the spearmint leaves in a teapot, and pour the boiling water over them. Cover and let them steep for 5 minutes.
3. Pour the tea through a strainer into the rinsed saucepan. Discard the spearmint leaves.
4. Add the sugar to the liquid and bring it to a boil.
5. Mix the cornstarch in the cold water. Add it to the soup, and simmer the soup 2 – 3 minutes while stirring until it clears and thickens.
6. Cool the soup to room temperature and refrigerate it 2 hours.
7. Before serving, squeeze a few drops of lime juice into the soup. Place a half slice of lime in each bowl.

Serves 4

Patty Pan Maple Soup (Chilled)

Authentic maple syrup lends a distinguished dessert flavor to this summer squash. Select the smaller patty pans, which haven't gone to seed. Other summer varieties, such as the ubiquitous zucchini, may be substituted and add a different color and flavor.

3 C patty pan (white scalloped) squash, chopped (approximately 4 – 5 small squashes)
1 ½ C water

1 t fresh lemon juice
½ C heavy cream
¼ C maple syrup

1. In a saucepan over high heat, bring the squash, water, and lemon juice to a boil.
2. Lower the heat, cover, and simmer for 5 – 7 minutes.

3. Drain the squash in a strainer, reserving the cooking liquid. Measure ¾ cup of cooking liquid, and place it in a blender container with the squash. Purée about 30 seconds.
4. Pour the purée into a bowl. Stir in the cream and maple syrup.
5. Refrigerate for at least 2 hours.

Serves 4

ॐ
PEACH SOUP (CHILLED)

The cornstarch will clear as it reaches the boiling point. Late summer, when the peach harvest is in full swing, is the best time for this soup.

2 T cornstarch
1 ½ C cold water
1 C white wine
1 t lemon juice
3 C fresh ripe peaches, peeled,
   pitted, and thinly sliced

¾ C maple syrup
½ C heavy cream
1 T sugar

1. Dissolve the cornstarch in the cold water at the bottom of a large saucepan.
2. Turn the burner to medium high, and add the wine and lemon juice to the pan. Stir the mixture well as you bring it to a boil.
3. Add the peaches and boil them, stirring constantly for 2 minutes.
4. Remove the soup from the burner, add the maple syrup, and let the soup cool at room temperature.
5. Refrigerate the soup for 2 hours.
6. Before serving, whip the cream, slowly adding the sugar as you whip it.
7. Cap each serving with whipped cream.

Serves 4

FRUIT AND NUT

Pear Buttermilk
Soup (Chilled)

Quick and easy to make — and very tasty. This is an elegant soup for a summer brunch.

2 egg yolks	1 t grated lemon peel
¼ C sugar	½ t vanilla extract
1 t fresh lemon juice	2 C buttermilk
1 t fresh lime juice	1 pear, peeled and cored

1. In a medium-size bowl, beat the yolks and sugar together until they turn creamy and pale yellow.
2. Blend in the lemon and lime juices, lemon peel, and vanilla.
3. Blend in the buttermilk.
4. Pour the mixture into a saucepan over medium heat, and stir while heating the soup 4 – 5 minutes. Do not boil.
5. Cut the pear into small pieces, and mix into the soup.
6. Cool to room temperature, and refrigerate it for at least 2 hours.

Serves 4

Persian Cucumber
Soup (Chilled)

If it is hot and muggy outside and you don't feel like cooking, try this refresher. It works like an oasis in the desert.

1 C hot water	Freshly ground black pepper
2 T golden raisins	2 C plain yogurt
1 C cucumber (tightly packed), peeled, seeded, and diced	½ C ice water
1 T olive oil	1 C heavy cream
1 t wine vinegar	3 T walnuts, chopped
1 t salt	1 T fresh dill, de-stemmed and minced (½ t dried crushed dill may be substituted)
2 T scallions (bottom 3 inches only), finely sliced	

1. Bring the water to a boil. Soak the raisins in the hot water for 1 hour to plump them. Drain them and set them aside.

2. Place the cucumber in a bowl and mix in the olive oil, wine vinegar, salt, and scallions. Twist the pepper mill 3 or 4 times over the bowl.
3. Place the yogurt, ice water, and heavy cream in a mixing bowl. Stir in the walnuts, dill, and cucumber mixture.
4. Add the softened raisins. Refrigerate the soup for 30 minutes or more. (The raisins tend to sink, so use a ladle to bring them up from the bottom.)

Serves 4

&

PINK GRAPEFRUIT
SOUP (CHILLED)

Beat the summer heat with this refreshing dessert soup. It's delicious in deep winter, too, when grapefruit season is at a peak.

2 C fresh pink grapefruit sec-
tions and juice (2 grapefruit)
2 T minute tapioca
2 T brown sugar

4 C fresh pink grapefruit juice
(4 grapefruit)
½ C heavy cream
1 T sugar

1. To section the grapefruit: peel away the rind and white inner integument. With a sharp knife, slice near each section membrane by pushing the knife toward the center of the fruit. The fruit should come loose in triangular sections. Reserve any juice, and add it to the sections.
2. In a large saucepan over high heat, stir the tapioca and sugar into 4 cups of grapefruit juice, along with the sections and their juice.
3. Boil the soup for 2 minutes, stirring occasionally. Remove it from the heat, and cool to room temperature.
4. Pour the soup in a bowl, and refrigerate it for at least 2 hours.
5. Chill the serving bowls. In a separate bowl whip the cream, slowly adding the sugar as it thickens.
6. Crown each portion with a mound of whipped cream.

Serves 4 – 6

PRUNE SOUP (CHILLED)

Prunes are high in iron and vitamin B6 and are a wonderful energy food. This soup exonerates prunes from a ho-hum stewed fruit role and livens their image as a first-class dessert.

1 C prunes, pitted	**Sprinkle of mace**
3 C water (to cover)	**1 T sour cream**
¼ C dark brown sugar	**½ C heavy cream**

1. In a saucepan, cover the prunes with the water and bring them to a boil. Cover the pan, turn off the heat, and let the prunes rehydrate for 45 minutes until they soften.
2. Drain the prunes, reserving the liquid (about 2 cups).
3. Place the liquid in a saucepan, add the sugar, and bring the contents to a boil. Cool.
4. Place the prunes in a blender, add the prune liquid and the mace, and blend for 2 minutes. Pour the purée into a bowl.
5. In a separate bowl, whip the sour cream into the heavy sweet cream. Fold it into the prune purée. Refrigerate for 2 hours. Serve in chilled cups or bowls.

Serves 4

PURPLE GRAPE SOUP (CHILLED)

Sparkling grape juice is available bottled or canned. It comes naturally fermented or with soda added. The spritz adds a light quality to this soup.

3 C purple grape juice	**¼ C cold water**
¼ C sugar	**½ C unsweetened sparkling**
1 T fresh lemon juice	**grape juice**
2 T cornstarch	

1. Place the grape juice, sugar, and lemon juice in a large saucepan. Bring the ingredients to a low boil, stirring to dissolve the sugar. Reduce the heat to a simmer.
2. In a measuring cup, mix the cornstarch in the water. Pour it slowly into the grape juice mixture and boil gently, stirring 2 – 3 minutes until it thickens and clears.
3. Cool to room temperature, and refrigerate the soup for 2 hours.
4. Immediately before serving, stir in the sparkling grape juice and ladle into individual bowls.

Serves 4 – 6

SOUPS

PURPLE PLUM SOUP (CHILLED)

After the soup is cool, you may purée it in a blender. We prefer the texture of the softened fruit, although the flavor remains the same — dark and delicious.

4 large purple plums
3–4 C water (to cover)
3 T dark brown sugar

⅛ t freshly grated nutmeg
2 T marsala

1. Drop the plums into boiling water for 3–4 minutes to loosen the skins. Drain them, reserving the cooking liquid. Peel off any remaining skins.
2. Cut the plums into small pieces, discarding the pits. Place the plum pieces in a saucepan with 2 cups of the reserved cooking liquid.
3. Add the sugar, nutmeg, and marsala. Cover the pan, and over high heat gently boil the soup for 10 minutes.
4. Cool it to room temperature, and refrigerate the soup for 2 hours.
5. Serve the soup in chilled cups or bowls.

Serves 4

RED RASPBERRY SOUP (CHILLED)

A scoop of whipped cream floating in each bowl adds a smooth contrast to the luscious tart flavor of the berries.

4 C red raspberries, hulled
2 C water
1 t fresh lemon juice
Sprinkle of allspice

3 ½ T sugar
1 T cassis (currant liqueur)
1 ½ T cornstarch
¼ C cold water

1. In a large saucepan over high heat, boil the raspberries in the water 3–4 minutes until they soften.
2. Pour the raspberries into a sieve over a large bowl. With a stainless steel spoon, press the juice from the berries. Retain the juice, and discard the raspberry pulp in the sieve.
3. Return the juice to the rinsed saucepan over medium heat.
4. Stir the lemon juice, allspice, sugar, and cassis into the simmering liquid.
5. In a measuring cup, mix the cornstarch into the cold water. Pour this mixture into the juice and boil gently for 2–3 minutes, stirring until the soup thickens and clears.
6. Cool the soup to room temperature, and refrigerate it at least 2 hours.

Serves 4

FRUIT AND NUT

RHUBARB STRAWBERRY
SOUP (CHILLED)

This soup contends for first place with strawberry-rhubarb pie.
Strawberries are just coming in when rhubarb is on the way out, so timing
is imperative if you want fresh fruits. Rhubarb leaves are poisonous. Use
the stalks only.

4 C rhubarb stalks (base knob removed), sliced	**½ C sugar**
2 C strawberries, hulled	**1 T cornstarch**
2 C water	**¼ C cold water**
1 slice lemon	**¼ C heavy cream**
1 T sweet red wine	**1 T sugar**

1. In a large saucepan over high heat bring the rhubarb, strawberries, and water to a boil. Simmer them for 5 – 8 minutes until they soften.
2. Pour the fruit into a large sieve placed over a bowl. With a stainless steel spoon, gently press the juice from the fruit, retaining the juice in the bowl and discarding the fruit pulp.
3. Return the juice to the rinsed saucepan. Add the lemon slice, wine, and sugar. Bring them to a simmer so that the sugar dissolves. With a slotted spoon, remove the lemon slice. Discard it.
4. In a measuring cup, mix the cornstarch in the cold water. Stir this mixture into the juice and boil the soup for 2 – 3 minutes, stirring until it thickens and clears.
5. Cool the soup to room temperature, and refrigerate it for 2 hours.
6. In a bowl whip the cream, slowly adding the sugar as the cream mounds.
7. Serve the soup in chilled bowls with a garnish of whipped cream.

Serves 4

RÖDGRÖD (CHILLED)

In our singular travels one of us landed in the Hartz Mountains, Germany, at an international conference. The Danish students took over the kitchen one day and produced Rödgröd, a fruit soup sounding like a disease and tasting like ambrosia. The delight of this soup is its variety of textures and blend of tastes. In smaller portions and without whipped cream, it may be served as an appetizer.

½ C raisins
½ C prunes, cooked, pitted, and chopped
½ C dried apricots, chopped
1 C dry red wine
2½ C cold water
1 lb prepared tart pitted cherries, with juice
2 tart cooking apples, peeled, cored, and diced

1 cinnamon stick
⅓ C sugar
4 t arrowroot (or 2 T cornstarch)
½ t grated orange or lemon rind
½ C heavy cream
1 T sugar
Sprinkle each of freshly grated nutmeg, ground cinnamon, and orange rind

1. Soak the raisins, prunes, and apricots in the red wine and 2 cups of cold water for 1 hour.
2. Place all the fruits in a large saucepan with the soaking liquid.
3. Add the cinnamon stick, ⅓ cup of sugar, and boil the ingredients for 10–15 minutes until the fruits soften. (The apples should be fairly firm.)
4. In a measuring cup, mix the arrowroot with remaining cup of cold water, and add this mixture to the soup.
5. Taste the soup, adjusting for sugar. Add the ½ grated orange rind.
6. Over high heat, bring the soup to a boil. Lower the heat and simmer the soup for 2–3 minutes, stirring until it thickens.
7. Cool the soup to room temperature, and refrigerate it for at least 2 hours.
8. In a bowl whip the cream, slowly adding the sugar as the cream mounds.
9. Serve in chilled glass bowls or compote cups with a scoop of whipped cream on each and a sprinkle of nutmeg, cinnamon, and orange rind.

Serves 6–8

FRUIT AND NUT

ROSE HIP SOUP

High in ascorbic acid, rose hips are the fruit of the rose. You may find them in most natural food stores. They look like dried cherries and have a marly odor to them. This fruit soup carries the day served either hot or chilled.

2 C dried rose hips	½ C semidried Turkish apricots
6½ C cold water	2 T arrowroot
¼ C lemon juice	½ C heavy cream, whipped
½ C honey	Freshly grated nutmeg

1. Place the rose hips in a saucepan. Cover them with 3 cups of water, bring them to a boil over high heat, and boil for 1 minute. Take them off the burner and cover them with a lid. Let them soak overnight. Don't remove the lid.
2. When they're ready to use, bring them to a boil with a further 3 cups of water. Reduce the heat, cover, and let them simmer for 45 minutes.
3. Strain the liquid into a bowl and discard the rose hips. You will have about 4½ cups of rose hip liquid.
4. Pour this liquid into a saucepan and add the lemon juice, honey, and apricots. Bring them to a boil over medium-high heat.
5. In a measuring cup, dissolve the arrowroot in the remaining ½ cup of water and add it to the boiling soup.
6. Lower the heat to medium and simmer the soup 8 – 10 minutes, stirring occasionally as the soup thickens and clears.
7. Serve the soup hot with a dollop of whipped cream and a fillip of freshly grated nutmeg.

Serves 6

RYE BREAD SOUP (CHILLED)

Chilled Rye Bread Soup *thickens into a pudding that has a pleasant substantial capacity. It makes a filling soup for those blustery cold days of winter. This is one soup equally delicious hot or chilled.*

2 5-oz boxes of rye rusks	peeled, cored, and thinly sliced
9 C boiling water	½ C red currant jelly
¼ C dark rum	¾ C dark brown sugar
¼ C golden raisins	Sprinkle of allspice
1½ C fresh or frozen cranberries	1 jigger (1½ oz) marsala
½ C water	½ C heavy cream
1½ C fresh cooking apples,	1 T sugar

1. Place the rusks in a large bowl and pour the boiling water over them. Let them soak for 5 minutes.
2. Pass the soaked rusks through the fine disc of a food mill into a bowl. Reserve the rusk purée.
3. In a small saucepan over high heat, add the rum to the raisins and bring them to a boil. Cover them and remove them from the heat so that they plump while you prepare the rest of the soup.
4. In a saucepan over high heat, boil the cranberries in ½ cup of water until they pop and soften. Pass the cranberries with the liquid through the fine disc of a food mill into another bowl.
5. In a large soup pot or Dutch oven, gently boil the cranberries, apples, currant jelly, sugar, allspice, and marsala for a few minutes. Stir in the rusk purée and raisins with the rum. Cover the soup and cook it for 15 minutes, stirring it occasionally to prevent sticking.
6. The soup will be of porridge consistency. Remove it from the burner, and remove the lid to cool the soup to room temperature. Refrigerate it, covered, for 3 hours.
7. When ready to serve, whip the cream in a bowl, slowly adding the sugar as it mounds. Crest each serving with the whipped cream.

Serves 6 – 8

&

SPICY PEAR SOUP

This thick, spicy dessert soup has many layers of taste blended into a single perky effect. It would complement a pork roast or roast duck dinner.

2 T sweet butter
⅓ C onion, peeled and diced
½ garlic clove, peeled, crushed, and minced
1 C celery, threaded and diced
1 T parsley, de-stemmed and minced
1 ½ t ground nutmeg
1 T fresh grated gingerroot

¼ t salt
¼ t allspice
⅔ C sweet white wine
⅔ C fresh orange juice
3 C fresh Anjou pears, peeled, cored, and chopped
⅓ C heavy cream
2 t Cointreau (orange-based liqueur)

1. In a heavy saucepan over medium heat, melt the butter.
2. Add the onion, garlic, celery, and parsley. Sauté them a few minutes in the butter. Cover and let them sweat 5 – 8 minutes, stirring occasionally so they don't brown.
3. Stir in the nutmeg, gingerroot, salt, and allspice.

4. Add the wine, orange juice, and pears. Simmer, covered, for approximately 25 minutes until the pears soften.
5. Place the pear mixture in a blender and purée them 1 minute.
6. Stir the cream and Cointreau into the pear purée. Heat but don't boil. Serve hot.

Serves 4–6

&

STRAWBERRY SOUP (CHILLED)

This recipe derives from Café la Fraise restaurant in Hanover, New Hampshire. They served it as an appetizer in an exquisite flat flowery soup plate. We prefer it as a dessert soup. Either way it's irresistible.

1 ½ C water
¾ C Bordeaux
½ C sugar
⅛ C lemon juice
⅛ t cinnamon

1 qt strawberries, hulled, washed, and puréed in a blender (reserve 2 whole berries)
½ C heavy cream
3 T sour cream

1. In a saucepan over medium heat, boil the water, Bordeaux wine, sugar, lemon juice, and cinnamon for 15 minutes, stirring occasionally.
2. Add the strawberry purée and simmer the soup for an additional 10 minutes, stirring frequently. Skim off any foam.
3. Cool the soup to room temperature, and refrigerate it for 2–3 hours until it is completely chilled.
4. Immediately before serving, whip the cream in a bowl and combine it with sour cream.
5. Fold this cream mixture into the chilled soup.
6. Garnish each serving with a strawberry half.

Serves 4

TANGERINE MANDARIN SOUP (CHILLED)

An old-fashioned nonelectric juice squeezer works best with tangerines. Otherwise, it's more difficult to extract the juice without including too much of the bitter pulp and rind. For gilding the lily, top Tangerine Mandarin Soup *with peaks of lightly sweetened whipped cream.*

2 ½ C fresh tangerine juice (about 1 ½ dozen tangerines)
2 cloves
1 C mandarin sections (11-oz can), with ⅔ of the juice

2 T cornstarch
6 T sugar
2 T Cointreau (orange-based liqueur)

1. Place the tangerine juice in a saucepan with the cloves.
2. Drain the mandarin orange sections, and reserve them in a bowl and the juice in another bowl.
3. Mix ⅔ cup of the mandarin juice with the cornstarch and sugar and add this mixture to the saucepan, bringing them to a boil.
4. Simmer the juices for 2–3 minutes, stirring constantly until the soup thickens and clears.
5. Cool the soup to room temperature, and add the reserved mandarin sections.
6. Refrigerate the soup for 2–3 hours. Remove the cloves and add the Cointreau before serving, stirring it well.

Serves 4

FRUIT AND NUT

White Grape Lemon Soup (Chilled)

This soup may be served between courses as a palate freshener. Or whip it up after a tiring day at work. It's easy, quick, and sensational.

4 C white grape juice
¼ C sugar
⅓ C golden raisins

¼ C almond slivers, toasted
2 T cornstarch
¼ C cold water
1 T fresh lemon juice

1. In a large heavy saucepan over high heat, boil the grape juice and sugar. Stir and simmer it for 2 – 3 minutes until the sugar dissolves.
2. Add the raisins and almonds. Simmer the soup 3 – 4 more minutes to plump the raisins.
3. In a measuring cup, mix the cornstarch in the cold water and stir it into the juice mixture. Bring it to a low boil 2 – 3 minutes, stirring constantly as the soup thickens and clears.
4. Add the lemon juice and cool the soup to room temperature.
5. Refrigerate the soup for 2 – 3 hours.

Serves 4

SOUPS

INDEX

211